Human Wholeness

Human Wholeness

A Spirituality of Relationship

Mark G. Boyer
and Matthew S. Ver Miller

WIPF & STOCK · Eugene, Oregon

HUMAN WHOLENESS
A Spirituality of Relationship

Wipf & Stock
An Imprint of Wipf and Stock Publishers
199 W. 8th Ave., Suite 3
Eugene, OR 97401

www.wipfandstock.com

ISBN 13: 978-1-4982-2036-1

Manufactured in the U.S.A.   02/25/2015

Dedicated to all those
whose relationships with each of us
enabled us to write this book,
especially Janna Ver Miller
and Jazer, Josiah, and Trevor Ver Miller.

The Master was an advocate both of learning and of Wisdom.

"Learning," he said when asked, "is gotten by reading books or listening to lectures."

"And Wisdom?"

"By reading the book that is you."

He added as an afterthought: "Not an easy task at all, for every minute of the day brings a new edition of the book!"

— ANTHONY DE MELLO, *ONE MINUTE WISDOM*

Contents

Preface

WHAT BEGAN MANY YEARS ago as mentor-mentee sessions between me, Mark G. Boyer, and Matthew S. Ver Miller, became a special relationship because the mentee, Ver Miller, decided that he wanted more than the mentor, I, was giving. Ver Miller once told me, "You're not going to get away."

The mentor taught the mentee how to reflect on the events of his life and learn not only his own truth, but to learn how to learn from what he experienced, that is, in the words of the epigraph above, to read the book that is he. The mentee turned the process around and began to assist the mentor in an exchange that, ultimately, led us to write this volume. By reading our words, you also share in our friendship which continues in the process of always becoming more than we who form it.

In Christian understanding, each person is created in the image and likeness of God. Thus, when two people enter into a friendship, each brings the image of God to the other so God is encountered in and through the other. In Hinduism this godself is called the atman, which once uncovered reveals the Brahmin, true self. Through its practices, Buddhism seeks nirvana, a person's true self in union with all that exists. The goal of Taoism is human wholeness through harmony or balance. In Judaism, a person finds wholeness by keeping covenant. In other words, all world religions have the goal of achieving human wholeness through relationships.

Our hope is that the reader will be assisted in seeing how the relationships he or she has are not mere human interactions, but occasions for also experiencing God in each other. The transcendent aspect of relationship has enabled us to discover God in each other and many other friends in our lives. We desire to share the wholeness we have experienced through the seven dimensions of human relating or connecting to each other. Through reflections and discussions about each dimension, we have discovered the freedom to become who we are in each other's presence and receive back the gift we offer to each other in total freedom. In other words, we have discovered, and continue to discover, our true selves by giving them away to each other.

Because we are Christians, we use Jesus as our model for human relating. Christianity claims that he was one hundred percent God and one hundred percent human. If such is the case, then he best illustrates how God meets God in human relating. Christianity names this as transcendence, which will be explored in these pages. We hope this book will serve to spark the reader's own reflections and make him or her more aware of the transcendent dimension of human relationships.

In addition to each other, many others have contributed to our understanding of friendship. In fact, every person we have befriended or who has befriended us has contributed to the writing of this book. Outstanding contributors include Jeremy Graddy, Thomas Pesek, and Janna Ver Miller. All are deep thinkers; none hesitated to share through dialogue his or her journey of growth in human wholeness and relationship with God.

There is more to human wholeness that we write about here. We cannot know what that more is because we are always in the process of becoming who we are. This work is a bookmark on our lifetime journey of relating that leads to human wholeness. We hope this serves as an empowering framework to foster continual increase in the experience of transcendence in interpersonal relationships and communion with the Divine. We hope it will assist you with your next step on your lifetime journey.

Mark G. Boyer
Matthew S. Ver Miller

Introduction

THIS BOOK PRESUMES THE experience of friendship. A friend is a person who is attached to another person by affection or esteem. A friend is a favored companion on the journey of life.

Most people would not dispute the fact that they have a variety of friends, who, on an imaginary scale, probably range from mere acquaintance to close friend, that is, from a superficial connection to one that shares relationship intimacy in the form of a very close association, familiarity, bond, belonging, and knowing. Relationship intimacy in friendships can consist of emotional, social, intellectual, recreational, nonsexual physical, experiential, and spiritual dimensions with someone of the same sex or the opposite sex.

A friendship may be defined by the environment in which it is formed. The work environment may define the friend. A national party affiliation may define the friend. Travel companion may define the friend. A friendship may transcend environment and grow over time. A long and warm association developed over years may define a close friend. Each individual psychologically creates categories of friends, and these may be similar or different from others' categories.

Friendship as an experience of God and as a path to God is not a new idea. After his conversion from Judaism to Christianity, Paul writes about having entered into such a deep friendship with Jesus that it was no longer he who lived, but it was Christ who lived in him. By quoting a hymn, Paul illustrates that everything was created in and through Christ, the only Son of God (cf. Col 1:15–20). Thus, everything is connected to God, and friendship gives us a glimpse of this connectivity.

Christian mystics often write about the connectedness that exists among all things that have their origin in God. Christian mystics believe God meets God in human relating. One way to experience such connectivity is friendship. Hildegard of Bingen writes that the Holy Spirit penetrates everything in the heavens, on the earth, and under the earth. She refers to this as "penetrated with connectedness" or "penetrated with relatedness." Meister Eckert, another famous mystic, argues that relation is the essence of everything that exists. Thomas Aquinas states that all things are united in friendship to each other and to God. Francis de Sales believed that God acted in ordinary human relationships, and that spiritual friendship, the culmination of human friendship, is necessary for a full Christian life. Thus, friendship can be an experience of God and a path to God.

Because Christian mystics see into the depths of friendship, they understand that every experience of love makes the beloved to be in the lover, and the lover is the beloved. In other words, there is a transparency that develops between friends. They can see through each other to the God who penetrates all things with the connectivity of the Holy Spirit.

One's awareness of such connectivity means that the love between friends brings about even deeper transparency. Friendship plumbs the depths of the other in a quest to find God. Those who love are directed not only toward themselves, but also toward others. However, love for one's self is a necessary foundation for friendship. Well-ordered self-love is right and natural (cf. Matt 19:19; 22:39). To know and to appreciate one's own worth is what is offered to another. Simultaneously, friends assist each other in knowing themselves, each other, and the God whose Spirit connects all things, even them.

Authentic, transparent friendship has no ulterior motives; it desires only to love the other person. Love is the acceptance of the other person as he or she is. Love respects the differences of the other; love honors the differences of the other. There is no desire on the part of either person to control or manipulate the other. The two people offer each other the freedom to flourish. Each person wishes the best for the other. Love enables each person to be transparent, vulnerable, and open to the other.

The full experience and expression of love implies physical presence. While a friendship can be maintained through the telephone or e-mail or texting or any other electronic means available, the transparency engendered by physical presence cannot be elicited any other way. When friends are in each other's physical presence, they express verbally and non verbally the degree of their love for each other.

The degree of love is based on the degree of free commitment. Each person is equal to the other, and this equality enables the freedom for each to make an equal response. This equality also enables each to put the other first. Thus, one willingly sacrifices himself or herself for the other. Furthermore, each friend learns about himself or herself through the transparency of the other. Love is a genuine care for the other that the other becomes all he or she can be; one cares for the other as he or she cares for himself or herself in freedom.

In other words, one person connects with another; the connection results in unity; such unity is the work of the Holy Spirit, who is God. Friendship is both an experience of God and a path to God through the other person.

In our experience, what often begin as mentor-mentee sessions can become friendships that are experiences of God. The mentor teaches the mentee how to reflect on the events of his or her life and learn not only his or her own truth, but learn how to learn from what he or she experiences, that is, to read the book that each is. Mentees often turn the process around and begin to assist the mentor in an exchange that leads to the mentor's further growth and development.

All relationships begin with some level and form of connectivity to at least one aspect of human wholeness. As both parties enter more deeply into their relationship, more connectivity is achieved in more of the seven aspects of human wholeness. Human wholeness continues to develop through the friendship. Human wholeness, as we define it, consists of seven dimensions of human relating that plumb the depths of shared connectivity. These aspects are intellectual, psychological, emotional, physical, sexual, spiritual, and aesthetic. Through shared reflections and discussions, friends discover the freedom to become who each is in the other's presence and receive back the gift each offers to the other in total freedom. In other words, friends discover their true selves by giving them away to each other.

Our hope is that the reader will be assisted in seeing how the relationships he or she has are not just mere human interactions, but occasions for also experiencing God. The transcendent aspect of relationship can enable friends to discover God in each other.

Mark G. Boyer
Matthew S. Ver Miller

Chapter 1

Human Wholeness
A Definition

IMAGINE A ROPE BRAIDED out of seven strands of twine, forming a circle so that even the ends of the rope are woven together. This is an image for the concept of human wholeness. A person functions most wholly when all seven strands of the aspects of his or her life are braided together tightly. These seven aspects of human wholeness form one complete person who is greater than the sum of his or her dimensions. We examine these seven aspects separately in order to come to a deeper understanding of each of them, but in the final analysis they are not disconnected. A person is not composed of aspects; a person is a whole being created in the image and likeness of God.

Human wholeness is a process of becoming. When a person is not becoming or growing, a knot occurs in the rope of human wholeness. That knot affects an aspect of human wholeness, but because of the interconnectivity of the person, it affects the whole person. Because human wholeness is a process of always becoming, it affects the person and all of his or her relationships.

A healthy relationship, one which is in the process of always becoming, not only brings to each of the two people relating a sense of wholeness, but it also fosters the wholeness of their relationship. Wholeness is a sense of well-being that permits people to flourish and find fulfillment in all of their seven primary dimensions: intellectual, psychological, emotional, physical, sexual, spiritual, and aesthetic.

The process of relating helps each person integrate these dimensions of self and realize wholeness. Relating is the process of living that reaches fulfillment by connecting with other people through the primary dimensions of being whole. It enables each person in the relationship to see himself or herself "embedded in the matrix of a grander entity, and to intuit connections to all other living things."[1]

Fowler, in his *Becoming Adult, Becoming Christian*, says, ". . . Human . . . wholeness . . . is . . . a way of being and moving, a way of being on pilgrimage."[2] Later, he says that wholeness is "the response a person makes with his or her total self to the address of God and to the calling to partnership."[3] Indeed, that is the realization of those who are friends, namely, that they are on a journey of self-discovery as they simultaneously discover the other, and, through the self and other, they discover God and enter into cooperation with each other and God.

The Matthean Jesus addresses wholeness when he tells his crowd of listeners, "Be perfect . . . as your heavenly Father is perfect" (Matt 5:48). The Greek word *tam*, translated as *perfect* refers to the wholeness of God. So, what Jesus tells the crowd is to be whole, like God is whole—not perfect in the usual sense of being without flaw.

As already stated above, we do not experience ourselves as dimensions or aspects, but in order to understand how one person connects to another we will explore the dimensions of human wholeness separately. We are not composed of pieces, like body and soul, body and spirit, sacred and secular. Each person is a whole human being. And his or her unique definition of wholeness will

1. Shlain, *The Alphabet*, 362.

2. Fowler, *Becoming Adult*, 74.

3. Ibid., 95.

vary from all others. This is to suggest that each person integrates differently these dimensions of a whole human self. The seven aspects interact to form wholeness in each person which resembles the wholeness in no one else.

The opening image invites the reader to image human wholeness as a rope circle braided out of seven strands of twine. Also, the seven aspects of wholeness are like circuits on a computer chip. To achieve optimum function, they must be integrated, experienced together as parts of a whole. We specify the dimensions of wholeness only to write about them. In the end, we must always return to wholeness. All we can do is name those primary aspects of human wholeness in an effort to explore the ways that they are distinct and yet connected to each other.

As people relate, they come to a deeper awareness of God's presence. Fowler, calling the process synergy, says:

> Synergy means the mingling of divine love with our capacities to love, guiding them and grounding them in the grace of God. Synergy means the release of a quality of creativity and energy that manifests our likeness to the restored image of God in us. Synergy means human beings fully alive and using the gift of our strengths and virtues in the service of the realization of the commonwealth of love.[4]

For us, then, wholeness is best understood as the lifetime process of cooperating with each other and God to bring these seven dimensions of ourselves into a unified human maturity. Integrated, the dimensions of self converge to form a wholeness, the self that one identifies with and offers to another in relationship, which flows outward to others and back again to those who engage in the process of relating.

4. Ibid., 141.

Dimensional Convergence

The dimensions of human wholeness overlap with each other in multiple ways, in varying degrees, and converge with each other in the process of integration toward wholeness. The amount of overlap differs from one person to another. However, even with the convergence, we can say that wholeness is greater than the individual alone. It is greater than one's personal wholeness because one's personal wholeness, which can never be complete, is always in the process of becoming—even beyond self. Shlain puts it this way: "Many of us have had experiences in which we seemed to glimpse other dimensions, or realities, and these epiphanies inspire the belief that there is an existence greater than the one commonly described."[5]

Human wholeness implies that each person in a relationship has a good understanding of his or her own possibilities and limitations imposed by personal endowments and the constraints and supports of environment. This is to suggest that each person has an identity, according to Fowler,

> an accrued awareness of oneself that maintains continuity with one's past meanings to others and to oneself and that integrates the images of oneself given by significant others with one's own inner feelings of who one is and of what one can do, all in such a way as to enable one to anticipate the future without undue anxiety about "losing" oneself.[6]

Covey calls this a "changeless core." He says, "The key to the ability to change is a changeless sense of who you are, what you are about and what you value."[7]

Wholeness flows out of each person to the other through relating because God calls each person to a wholeness which is greater than anyone can even begin to imagine. That wholeness is God's grace, the Holy One's self. In Fowler's words, we come to

5. Shlain, *The Alphabet*, 362.
6. Fowler, *Stages*, 77.
7. Covey, *Daily Reflections*, 40.

understand "that things are organically related to each other" and we attend "to the pattern of interrelatedness in things."[8]

Intellectual Aspect

The intellectual aspect of human wholeness is its mental facet, usually associated with the brain. It is the human need to study, to learn, to read, to reflect, to discuss, and to think about challenging ideas, and enhance or alter previously held concepts. When two people connect intellectually, they exchange ideas. They may read a book together, attend a class or lecture or educational program. They may watch a program on TV and discuss it or listen to a radio show and share ideas about it. A film may present the opportunity to engage in intellectual exchange.

Before two people can connect in the intellectual dimension, each must have progressed from a learning-for-the-sake-of-learning point to a learning-for-the-sake-of-self point. In the former, what a person studies doesn't penetrate him or her. It doesn't effect change. In the latter, what is learned is put into practice and integrated. The person is always in the process of changing because he or she is simultaneously in the process of learning. The former is often referred to as memorizing. The latter is learning that enables one person to teach another how to learn.

An important part of the intellectual connection is dialogue, not mere conversations, but genuine openness of each person to the concerns of the other. Dialogue implies that both people are actively listening and attending to what each says, not attempting to impose ideas or correct what the other speaks. Each person internalizes the viewpoint of the other in order to enhance his or her own and their mutual understanding. Ideas are reformed and distilled through dialogue. Because each person brings a unique point of view or perspective to the relationship, through dialogue each comes to respect the other's point of view, even if he or she doesn't totally grasp it at the time nor have the experience to

8. Fowler, *Stages*, 185.

validate it or agree with it. Indeed, disagreement does not inhibit the intellectual connection, but enhances it. The bottom line is that two people can agree that they disagree.

As information is shared, instead of seeking closure through dialogue, two people realize there are many perspectives on the idea, issue, or concept being shared. Probing, questioning, and the free exchange of ideas allows each person the freedom to learn from the other. The idea, issue, or concept may remain open for dialogue throughout the relationship. In other words, ambiguity is embraced and leads to endless exploration.

Dialogues lead to a deeper understanding not only of the other person's ideas, but to a deeper understanding of the other person. Dialogue forges a bond between two people, an intellectual connection, grounded in each person's authenticity as a learner.

Psychological Aspect

The psychological aspect refers to the study of the human soul or mind. It explores the true being or inner self of a person. It is associated with the mind, heart, or eye of the soul. The psychological aspect addresses the need for one human being to connect, bond, relate, and share with another. It assumes the need to know one's self through awareness and consciousness and be known through disclosure of one's self.

The psychological aspect suggests the need to share one's aspirations, hopes, fears, questions, insecurities, strengths, failures, and successes. It requires a secure foundation of trust in a relationship for mutual disclosure to occur without fear of shame, guilt, or embarrassment. The psychological dimension of a person is the ability to see one's self in the perspective of the long-range plan of one's life and be in the process of implementing it. It includes the ability to sacrifice what one immediately desires for a greater, future desire. In other words, a person is able to live a disciplined life and delay gratification for a greater good.

The psychological aspect of the self enables the human person to accept, understand, and critique what is received from another and to better understand who he or she is—what Fowler calls "images of the self."[9] In other words, one person connects to another through the self-image that he or she is able to share, even as it is always in the process of becoming, the process of change, the process of development.

The psychological dimension of a friendship is that which motivates one to present himself or herself as he or she is to another. It is the driving force, the psychic energy wanting to be given and received. However, one cannot be a good friend until one knows one's self. A healthy relationship requires two people who have achieved a level of self-security and are able to move outside of self and toward the other freely. One's self-image or self-identity dictates how comfortable one is in presenting himself or herself to another, that is, securely getting outside of self in order to move toward another in freedom.

Encompassing the manner in which we approach life and relationships, the psychological aspect of self requires that one identifies and faces his or her insecurity, which then offers one the secure insecurity or freedom to move out of self and toward another person. The more we know and understand ourselves, the greater our security. The greater our personal or self-security, the greater the freedom we experience to be, to express, and to develop who we are. This process creates an ever-widening spiral-pattern: self-understanding, self-security, freedom, etc. The way one is comfortable with and knows self is what he or she brings to any relationship.

Closely aligned to the psychological connection that occurs in a relationship is each person's unique personality, that which encompasses or defines one's totality, such as types, traits, strengths, and growth areas. To be able to synthesize and conceptualize who one is must be accomplished to some degree before a relationship can grow. In other words, a level of self-definition and identity are needed before entering into a healthy, productive relationship, which, in turn, further fosters self-security.

9. Ibid., *Becoming Adult*, 24.

The psychological aspect also deals with attitude, motivation, one's world views, and perspective. It involves the ability and willingness to critique the feedback one receives from friends by deciding to change or stay the same. With a personal interest and investment in psychological growth, one person attempts to see himself or herself through the other's eyes. This leads to a deeper sense of self-awareness and self-actualization, which, in turn, leads one to a decision to expand self or leave self alone. A relationship fosters the security to trust the authenticity of the other's seeing with the deepest respect for the other's openness to self.

When two people in a relationship are psychologically connected, both are willing to hear what the other heard, see what the other saw, and understand from the other's point of view. Such self-perception, how others see one, enables a person to know self from the other's perspective and attain some degree of self-objectivity and self-differentiation. As we get to know ourselves through another's hearing, seeing, and understanding, we also get to know the other better, too.

As one gets to know himself or herself as another knows him or her, one becomes more aware of how he or she comes across or is perceived by others. One of the results of the psychological connection is this: As one gets to know self, and as one gets to know the other, one gets to know self through the other. Thus, two points of view about self and one point of view about the other are gleaned from the psychological connection.

We can also speak of this using the image of a mirror. The other is a reflection of one, just as one is a reflection of the other. The sage in the Hebrew Bible (Old Testament) Book of Proverbs says, "Just as water reflects the face, so one human heart reflects another" (27:19). As the spiral of security widens—as we get more comfortable seeing ourselves in each other's reflection—we discover our commonalities, the basic ones consisting of existence and being created in the image of God. We also discover our differences—no one person can adequately reflect the other, because no two people are alike. Even twins differ psychologically. Learning about self takes place both through the ways two people are alike and different.

Likewise, self-security is achieved through the mutual sharing of alikenesses and differences. Both alikenesses and differences help us see beyond our own image—what we see when we look in the mirror—so that we can see more. Both alikenesses and differences disclose truth to those who freely relate. That truth, in turn, widens the perspective even more. Thus, what we perceive to be as an alikeness or a difference can provide the stability or security needed for self as it is in the process of change or becoming. Or to use the mirror image, both alikenesses and differences between two people in a relationship can reflect awareness, which is required for both stability and change.

Emotional Aspect

The emotional dimension of human wholeness refers to how a human being feels about self and others. It is associated with the heart, the inner core of whom we are, and the place where we are most familiar with ourselves. A healthy emotional level of development means that people are able to keep the commitments they make to themselves. Emotions influence one's attitude about or perspective on life, which, in turn, affects behavior. Fowler says that the emotional dimension refers to ideas which are learned and critiqued "in the sense of a deep-going, pervasive, and long-lasting set of fundamental dispositions of the heart."[10]

The realm of emotions, such "dispositions of the heart," include love, anger, sadness, happiness, depression, joy, anxiety, fear, etc. Emotions can be motivators for action or the lack thereof. They can serve as motivators for opening up one's world, if one is aware of them; or they can serve as motivators for closing off one's world, if one is not aware of them. Emotions cannot be controlled in the sense that people say they will stop feeling fear, for example. But emotions can be controlled by not predicating behavior to feelings

10. Ibid., 118.

but to one's set of values. Values stemming from rational thought and the choice to live consciously should dictate behavior.

Stated in another way, the emotional dimension of self represents the human primal response to stimuli which fosters and/or dictates behavior. The degree that the emotion is felt affects the decision about what to do (behavior) or not to do. Behavior based on emotions can be as erratic as the emotions themselves. That is why emotions must be critiqued in light of the appropriateness of one's response based on the values which dictate one's behavior.

As a relationship deepens between two people, the emotional defensiveness of both parties continues to dissipate. In a healthy relationship, both people set each other free and assist the other in critiquing emotions by raising the other's awareness of how he or she is responding to the emotion instead of his or her set of values. The trust that exists in a relationship allows both people to accept the emotional challenge without being defensive. When so engaged, personal emotional awareness is raised and the individual learns from the challenge instead of closing off himself or herself—or worse, basing his or her behavior on the emotion.

Any emotion that is shared in a healthy relationship means that the friendship is simultaneously enriched and diminished. The person offering it to the other is diminished, and the person receiving it is enriched. But when the person diminished by sharing receives from the one originally receiving, both parties are changed and the self-awareness of both as a gift is more deeply experienced.

Sometimes, after sharing an emotion, one must wait for a response from the other. The other chooses the proper time, place, or occasion to share his or her emotion. Genuine authenticity enables the other to recognize the right time, place, and occasion to express his or her feelings, while the one who first shared emotions respects the values of the other to such a degree that he or she is able to let the other take all the time he or she needs to respond. "For everything there is a season, and a time for every matter under heaven," observes the author of the Hebrew Bible (Old Testament) Book of Ecclesiastes (3:1).

The expressing of emotions presumes the ability of the people involved in a relationship to accept their own and the other's vulnerability. The degree that each is comfortable with self-vulnerability is the degree of the emotional transparency each can bring to the relationship.

As emotions are exchanged, a friendship increases in the sharing of the emotions of love and intimacy. The degree of expressing emotions is congruent to the level of intimacy, as that which forms the innermost character of a person is disclosed. The dialectic of the relationship implies that as one person expresses his or her emotions, he or she frees the other to do the same—whenever the other is ready.

To be human is to share emotions. The emotional dimension is one aspect of human beings that calls for expression. In other words, sharing feelings with another person is part of our nature. While emotions can be left unexpressed—often referred to as keeping them bottled up—no personal awareness in terms of self-knowledge develops. Only when they are expressed to another is the other's self-awareness raised and self-knowledge enhanced. To relate emotionally, to connect with another emotionally, is a dimension of being human. Emotional growth in terms of self-awareness is just as important as development in any other human dimension.

What two people in a relationship desire of each other is the ability to better identify and express their emotions. In other words, both people want to understand self as deeply as possible. Thus, each shares the dual role of guide and articulator for the other.

Prayer may be one of the best means of sharing emotions. Certainly, in prayer to God we express our feelings and remain open to God's response, just like we do in our human relationships. When we pray together, our emotions can either foster self-protection or self-disclosure. When self-protection occurs, little or nothing is shared, but when disclosure takes place through prayer, we give and receive life through our emotions. They are transmitters of life. The Johannine Jesus says he came that people "may have life, and have it abundantly" (John 10:10). Or as the Matthean Jesus puts it, ". . . Where two or three are gathered in my name, I am there among them" (Matt 18:20).

People share emotions through communication, that is, talking, telling their personal stories to each other, communing with words. They share emotions through prayer; intentional presence, that is, being proximate in space; eye contact; body language; camaraderie, that is, the freedom needed to be in another's presence and inhabit his or her space; love; and silence, which can envelope those relating and set them free.

Reverential touch, that is, human contact that offers comfort, care, compassion, healing, love, sharing in suffering, and communion with the other, may be the greatest means of one person connecting to the emotional dimension of another. With the greatest respect for the other and without any intention to harm him or her, one's body becomes the conduit for emotional self-revelation.

Chittister says, "What we hold in our hearts for a person is the way we'll act" toward him or her.[11] The emotion named compassion "comes out of our ability to accept ourselves,"[12] says Chittister. Compassion "makes us most like God,"[13] she says. "To be without compassion is to fail to know the self. When we recognize and accept our own frailties, we have no trouble dealing tenderly with the needs and the lapses of others,"[14] states Chittister.

Physical Aspect

The physical aspect is associated with the bodily features of each person. It especially associated with the eyes, face, and hands. The need to eat, exercise, recreate, and touch are aspects of human physicality or bodiliness. Coll says that we are more "embodied

---

11. Chittister, "Monastic Way."

12. Ibid.

13. Ibid.

14. Ibid.

spirits than . . . enspirited bodies."[15] By relating one embodied spirit is present to another. In other words, the physical body, a reflection of God's Spirit, "the breath of life" (Gen 2:7), makes every person "a living being" (Gen 2:7). In his second letter to the Corinthians, Paul refers to our "embodied spirits" as earthen vessels which hold "this treasure in clay jars, so that it may be made clear that this extraordinary power belongs to God and does not come from us" (2 Cor 4:7). When one person is physically present to another, both share Spirit through their bodies. Buber says, ". . . As soon as we touch a You, we are touched by a breath of eternal life."[16]

Two people relating make physical contact with each other in many ways. Indeed, a healthy relationship both asks for and allows for some forms of physical contact. The freedom engendered through relationship allows each person to be physically authentic in the presence of the other. This same freedom also allows for the placement of boundaries for the physical. What is appropriate physical contact between the two people is discussed and defined by them, and it may change over time. The boundaries of physical contact enjoyed by those relating will differ from one relationship to another.

We can share our bodiliness through a handshake, a hug, or a pat on the back. The personal space of both people opens up to let the other in. We have no fear of the other invading our physicality because the trust engendered through the establishment of boundaries sets us free to welcome the other into our physical space and share our embodied spirits.

Looking deeply into the eyes of the other is another way we connect physically. Face-to-face encounters may be one of the best experiences of how one person brings the presence of God to the other person. The Holy One meets God as embodied spirit and reveals who he is through and to the two people who are relating. Face-to-face eye contact may be the best means of presenting the transparent self to the other.

15. Coll, *Christianity & Feminism*, 174.
16. Buber, *I & Thou*, 113.

The physical contact of gazing deeply into the eyes of the other can be a threatening experience for some people, who experience it as an invasion of personal space. Thus, being able to prolong eye contact requires a degree of intimacy between those relating. It is a comfortability factor flowing from the trust that both persons have in each other. Trust dissipates fear of the other person, and no threat is perceived. Both people relate to each other on the same level of trust with no intimidation caused by personal power, status, position, age, etc.

Physical contact is also experienced through recreational activity. Some people foster a relationship by working out, jogging, walking, hiking, swimming, or biking together. Keeping the embodied spirit in shape through a balanced diet, proper nutrition, and exercise enables one to be healthy and, consequently, feel good about self. Morneau says that physicality concerns how well "we manage our health by proper exercise and nutrition, by watching our weight, by taking or allowing time for leisure."[17] Relationships develop when people spend and share time together physically in each other's presence with no personal agendas of what needs to take place.

The physical connection can also be made through tears of joy and sadness. When one person receives the expression of emotion through tears, he or she honors and accepts the joy or sadness of the other. It is a privilege to share the tears of the other, much like sharing the prayer of the other by holding hands. Through prayer, two people not only connect physically but spiritually and share their embodied spirits with each other.

Such reverential touching, as in healing, displaying care, assisting during illness, can become a powerful connection between friends. In many cases, what is labeled care-giving becomes one skilled person assisting another nonskilled person. However, authentic care-giving touch empowers the other to recovery because there is no present threat of taking his or her independence away. Authentic care-giving shares the Spirit, the being, the grace that each possesses with the other and empowers the sick to speedier

17. Morneau, "Garden," 35.

healing. When touch is not genuine, it disempowers the individual receiving the care-giving. It takes away his or her independence and dignity and humiliates the one who cannot take care of himself or herself.

In Christian practice, every sacramental celebration contains an empowering touch to the embodied spirit. When baptizing, the minister, holding the individual, submerges the person who is buried with Christ "by baptism into death" (Rom 6:4) and then raises him or her to "newness of life" (Rom 6:4). When confirming, the minister not only lays an empowering hand on the head of the person, but anoints him or her with healing, sweet-smelling oil. Dorr says that people "want a faith that brings a sense of wholeness, a healing of the total person—the embodied spirit."[18] They also want relationships that empower them toward wholeness.

When people celebrate forgiveness in the sacrament of penance, the minister lays his forgiving hands on their heads. Likewise, when anointing the sick with healing oil, the minister lays his hands on the ill person's head and anoints his or her head and hands. For each of the three degrees of holy orders—deacon, priest, bishop—the ordaining bishop lays his hands on the head of the candidate and empowers the embodied spirit to ministry.

But maybe it is when they share meals that two people bring their mutual presence to a crescendo. When we share a meal, we share each other through the media of food and drink. Fellowship involves eating of each other through physical food and drink. For Christians, the Lord's Supper, Eucharist, involves not only the mutual embodied spirit sharing of all gathered around the table, but the simultaneous eating and drinking of the body and blood of Christ present in bread, food, and wine, drink. If the cliché is true that we become what we eat, then when two friends share a meal, they become the other, just like those who partake of the Lord's Supper become Christ's body. Writing to the Corinthians, Paul tells his readers, ". . . You are the body of Christ and individually members of it" (1 Cor 12:27).

18. Dorr, *Spirituality*, 29.

One unique physical characteristic is the voice. We use our vocal cords to create words to communicate with the other. Those relating recognize the other's voice and its tones and rhythms. In John's Gospel, Jesus compares himself to a shepherd who cares for the sheep. Then, he says that the sheep follow the shepherd "because they know his voice" (John 10:4). Likewise, two embodied spirits hear each other's voice and come to know and trust each other.

Because we are embodied spirits, the body cannot totally define who we are. In other words, we are much more than a body, which contributes to and fosters a healthy self-image. In fact, we think that people need a healthy self-image in order to trust the other so that they can connect physically. Without a healthy self-image, self- consciousness sets in and one is unable to move physically toward another. The self-understanding of who each person is in a relationship enables each to convey who he or she is physically without fear of embarrassment. In other words, one is able to be both physically and metaphorically naked in the presence of the other and not be ashamed.

Through the physical connection we transcend ourselves and make contact with the other at the deepest core of who each person is. Of course, one can get only as close as the other will let him or her. Self-revelation, however, enables embodied spirits to connect, and God shines through the connection. Dorr says, "Some deep instinct leads [us] to reject the kind of dualism that separates the spirit from the body . . . ."[19] It is through the physical that we experience the union of spirit and body connection to the union of spirit and body in another.

While the best kind of presence is physical presence, it is impossible for one person always to be physically in the presence of the other. But a "physical presence in absence" is possible. This "physical presence in absence" emerges from the physical presence in silence that two people have shared through their friendship. Just like the physical connection can take place only in absolute freedom, so "the physical presence in absence" can take place only

19. Ibid., 28-29.

16

in absolute freedom. In the absence of the physical presence of the other, we can experience the other, still remember what our bodily connection means, and still feel what our physical communion evoked emotionally. "Physical presence in absence" can be sparked by a memory, a photograph, or a song that binds or connects us to the person with whom we share a relationship.

Sexual Aspect

While it could be a corollary to the physical, the sexual is treated separately because of the male or female identity it offers to a human being. We note two aspects to the sexual dimension—gender and physicality—and understand that the physical quality of sexuality flows from gender even as gender is identified through the physical. The sexual dimension is associated with the primary and secondary sexual characteristics.

Even before we are able to discern that there are two human genders, we are "genderized" by the people around us. Boys are wrapped in a blue blanket or wear a blue wrist band. Girls are wrapped in a pink blanket or wear a pink wrist band. When adults approach a baby, they may often ask the parents, "Is it a boy or a girl?" and proceed to interact with the child based on what gender information is given. Later in life, toys, music, clothes, hair length, voice, body hair, and physical strength will further serve to identify male and female and distinguish one from another.

Gender affects the presence of two people. Cultural mores and taboos dictate behavior. One male is cautious of how he approaches another male, how he greets him, and if and where he touches him. A female approaches another female in a different manner. With less restraint, one woman will greet another and maybe hug or kiss her. And a male-female relationship has its own gender-dictated behavior, such as who drives the car when both are together. Does he open doors for her? Does she want him to pull out her chair when they eat in a restaurant?

In his first letter to the Corinthians, Paul declares, "In the Lord woman is not independent of man or man independent of woman. For just as woman came from man, so man comes through woman; but all things come from God" (11:11–12). Immediately before this, he discusses gender differences in the first century CE. He says that they are part of God's plan for humanity and should be maintained as significant. Indeed, we cannot separate gender from a person; one is either male or female. This is why Coll maintains that "sexuality . . . involves more than genitalia; it involves our whole being as male or female."[20]

From the human end of the sexual continuum to the divine end, gender gradually fades in importance. But on the human end it enables the freedom for two people to relate, and it facilitates the openness required for authentic communication. For example, one man will discuss with another man what he wouldn't discuss with a woman. One woman will share with another woman what she wouldn't share with a man. And in a male-female relationship two people will dialogue with each other about that which a male-male or female-female relationship would have little interest.

Gender also dictates for what two people are searching—friendship, companionship, marriage, intimacy, etc. It serves as one of the nuances of human relating. In other words, one cannot relate neutrally; one can relate only as a male or a female. While gender becomes less important as friendship grows deeper and has less affect on the people relating, it never disappears. Gender has an inevitable influence.

What is required for one adult to connect through gender with another? What is required is a choice to love in the sense that Paul uses the word *love* when he writes to the Romans. "Owe no one anything, except to love one another," states Paul, "for the one who loves another has fulfilled the law" (Rom 13:8). In general, people are mature enough to enter into this type of love relationship sometime from their mid to late twenties. They seem to move out of a preoccupation with the intense physical and sexual aspect accompanying the teenage years into a greater appreciation for the gender aspect.

20. Coll, *Christianity & Feminism*, 176.

Mature sexual adults value gender and are not afraid to explore its implications for themselves. They categorize unique gender differences and develop a respect for both their own and the opposite gender. They may often bond more deeply with members of the same sex, discovering an affinity, a basis of alikeness—which drives same sex friendships and names what they value in their own gender. Adults also appreciate the mystery of the opposite gender which drives the male-female or female-male relationship. The desire to know the opposite gender, to get into the opposite skin, as it were, makes a person want to experience that which he or she isn't. This deep respect for gender opens a new world which enables one to view himself or herself from a different perspective.

In Mark's Gospel, Jesus first emphasizes gender, saying, ". . . From the beginning of creation, 'God made them male and female.'" Then he emphasizes the physical, saying, "'The two shall become one flesh.' So they are no longer two, but one flesh" (Mark 10:6, 8). The connection between the male and female is so intense and intimate that they momentarily transcend their individuality and become one. The intention of those relating physically is what we commonly refer to as "having sex" or "making love." But it is much more than just the physiological process of reaching climax. It is a culmination of all the two have assisted each other to become up to that point in their lives. No boundaries remain. The two become one flesh.

In a male-female or female-male sexual, physical relationship, gender does not disappear. Indeed, it forms the basis for sexual expression and spans the lifetime of those relating. Both individuals continue to grow in greater understanding of being male and female even as they grow together as one. As their understanding grows, they change, and many of the roles socially engendered by gender fade away.

Gender gives us an identity which is always in the process of becoming through relationships. Coll captures this idea when she states, "Sexuality involves our self image, our self esteem, our very self.[21]" We must remember that the sexual is but one dimension of

21. Ibid., 177.

relating. According to Coll, "Sexuality is not to be equated with the whole of our personhood, but it is a basic and wondrous dimension of that personhood."[22]

Spiritual Aspect

The spiritual (not spirituality) dimension of wholeness refers to one's contact with the Divine or the Divine's contact with the human. The spiritual is associated with soul, spirit, and heart. The spiritual may also be associated with presence, air, up in the sky, as well as places of worship or reflection. Christian tradition understands that God makes the first move toward human beings both through creation and through grace. Morneau says the spiritual is "the gift dimension, . . . the working of grace, God's free bestowal of love and light into our soul."[23] Once we respond to God's invitation and begin to cooperate, we realize, as Mitchell states, that "we receive our being and life only by offering them back to their Source, just as we gain our humanity only by accepting God's gracious self-bestowal in the person of Jesus."[24] Fowler refers to the depth of cooperation with the Holy One as "human partnership in the work of God."[25]

Merton says

> that the will of God is not a "fate" to which we submit but a creative act in our life producing something absolutely new (or failing to do so), something hitherto unforeseen by the laws and established patterns. Our cooperation (seeking first the Kingdom of God) consists not solely in conforming to laws but in opening our wills out to this creative act, which must be retrieved in and by us—by the will of God.[26]

22. Ibid., 175.

23. Morneau, "Garden," 36.

24. Mitchell, "Amen," 251.

25. Fowler, *Becoming Adult*, 89.

26. Merton, *Intimate Merton*, 128.

He adds, "God gives us the freedom to create our own lives, according to His will, that is to say in the circumstances in which He has placed us."[27]

Two individuals bring their personal cooperation with God to their friendship. Each person's individual dimension of the process enhances the relationship dimension, and the relationship aspect, in turn, enhances the individual aspect.

God desires that we become whole human beings so that we can participate fully in the relationship God offers us. Through a friendship, two people each bring their individual growth in the God-human relationship to each other, completing the cycle of grace. God's gift of self to individuals is given away or shared with others. In other words, whole people desire to share with others what God has shared with them. Grace prompts the sharing of grace; gift-giving prompts gift-giving. We cannot contain God's grace; it overflows to others.

Individual cooperation with God involves prayer—both talking and listening to God. Such dialogue may take place not only through communication with God, but through talking and listening to others, especially those with whom we relate. It may also occur in the silence and wonder of creation. Prayer is the name we give to the process of relating with God. Merton, addressing God in prayer, writes, "Prayer is what you bring—for prayer is your gift to us rather than what you ask of us."[28] It includes whatever stimulates the human-divine partnership. And just as sharing with another usually erupts in praise of the other, so does prayer lead to praise of God. According to Mitchell, "We become ourselves only in the act of praising God."[29]

Every relationship is an undeserved gift, just like our individual invitation to partnership by God is an undeserved gift. Neither can be possessed by the other, because to do so would violate the very understanding of gift—that which is freely given away. Ownership, possession, or fear stops the opening process fostered

27. Ibid., 167.
28. Ibid., 114.
29. Mitchell, "Amen," 254.

by the gift. When sharing one's spiritual dimension with another through relationship, one does not transfer ownership, but gives away the grace that God has given away to him or her, thus completing the process of grace. "In the world of Spirit there is no scarcity," says Shea.[30] Each person becomes "a *pneumataphoros*, that is, a bearer of the Spirit."[31]

Reflecting on grace, Merton writes:

> I am the utter poverty of God. I am His emptiness, littleness, nothingness, lostness. When this is understood, my life in His freedom, the self-emptying of God in me is the fullness of grace. [It is] a love for God that knows no reason because He is the fullness of grace. [It is] a love for God that knows no reason because He is God, a love without measure, a love for God as personal.[32]

Instead of understanding the spiritual dimension as grace, some people prefer to speak of it as love, an intense desire to know another as well as one knows one's self. In his first letter, John exhorts his readers, writing, "Beloved, let us love one another, because love is from God; everyone who loves is born of God and knows God. . . . God is love" (1 John 4:7–8). God loves us first, and we respond individually by loving God and loving others. "We love because [God] first loved us," writes John (1 John 4:19). Because it originates in God, love is one of the deepest realities that human beings can experience. It is also one that once we experience it leaves us changed forever. "There is something completely permanent and irrevocable in our lives: The love that we have known in each other, that has changed us, that will remain with us in a hidden and transfigured—transfiguring—presence," says Merton.[33]

Through a friendship, two people share both divine and human love. They offer to each other the love that God offers to them individually, and they offer to each other the love that each has for the other. In other words, love overflows. First, it overflows from

30. Shea, "Eucharist," 115.

31. *Holy Spirit*, 67.

32. Merton, *Intimate Merton*, 328.

33. Ibid., 297.

God to individual people. Second, it overflows from one person to another. Third, it overflows from relationships to the communities to which one belongs.

Human love mirrors divine love and is required for an adult relationship. When two individuals decide to relate, both simultaneously accept that they are loved by and worthy of the love that comes from God and the other. Love once offered and accepted sparks a response from the receiver to give more love than he or she originally received. Thus, every act of love begets more love through the very freedom love engenders in relating. Comparing this spiraling process to a single wheat seed, the Johannine Jesus states, ". . . Unless a grain of wheat falls into the earth and dies, it remains just a single grain; but if it dies, it bears much fruit" (John 12:24). Sharing love with another is a type of death to self which results in more life.

When divine-human love is exchanged between two people, they also share their individual blessings from God, God's activity in their lives, the wisdom, truth, insight, and joy that they have experienced. What is shared is considered precious and is mutually respected because both unconditionally accept the other as he or she is. Both are open to all the possibilities of who the other is. Those who truly love do not attempt to change or manipulate the beloved. Authentic love sets the other free to be who he or she was, is, and will become. John makes this clear, stating, "There is no fear in love, but perfect love casts out fear . . ." (1 John 4:18). No one can put limits on love; to do so is to violate its gift-quality.

We are most like God when we give away what God has given to us. ". . . Since God loved us so much," writes John, "we also ought to love one another" (1 John 4:11). That is why Jesus summarized the spiritual dimension of human beings with one word—love. ". . . You shall love the Lord your God with all your heart, and with all your soul, and with all your mind, and with all your strength. You shall love your neighbor as yourself," states the Markan Jesus (Mark 12:30–31). It is with our totality, who we are, that we respond to God's love and share that love with others. "God is love, and those who abide in love abide in God, and God abides in them," says John (1 John 4:16).

Merton says, "Love is the door to eternity. He who loves is playing on the doorsteps of eternity, and before anything can happen, Love will have drawn him over the sill and closed the door."[34]

John continues, writing, "By this we know that we abide in [God] and he in us, because he has given us of his Spirit" (1 John 4:13). In the Christian Trinitarian tradition, the Spirit is understood to be engendered by the eternal love that the Father has for the Son. The Spirit is God's intimate life shared through God's own relating. Likewise, when two people create a relationship, they desire to know and be known by the other. This is nothing other than the desire to share the Spirit with each other that God has shared with each of them individually.

The Spirit flows through two people freely. The Johannine Jesus tells Nicodemus that the Spirit is like wind. "The wind blows where it chooses, and you hear the sound of it, but you do not know where it comes from or where it goes. So it is with everyone who is born of the Spirit" (John 3:8).

We can also compare the movement of the Spirit between people to electricity. The Spirit is the cord connecting them so that both receive and send life. This receiving-sending of the Spirit engenders life, love, and grace in those who relate, just like it does in the Trinity.

When two people connect through the spiritual dimension, they assist each other in tuning in to all the Spirit that God offers to them. Like radio waves that are always present, one helps another to achieve clear reception. And through the course of the relationship, this dialectic continues so that both get the full effect of the waves—the clearest reception of God's Spirit through each other. By assisting another, we also assist ourselves to open to the fullness of the love shared by the Father and Son.

Like the other dimensions of a relationship, the spiritual is a process never having a clear definition. It is an adventure of a lifetime. It is never complete until death, because one can never know

34. Ibid., 60.

the possibilities of what partnership with God may entail. Through a relationship, however, two people can connect to their spiritual dimensions through worship, Scripture reading, spiritual reading, television, movie, radio, and electronic exchanges. Anything that allows a friendship to connect spiritually deepens individual wholeness and the wholeness of the relationship.

Aesthetic Aspect

The aesthetic dimension of human wholeness concerns an appreciation for beauty or what is deemed to be beautiful. The aesthetic is associated with the senses, soul, and heart. Because philosophers have written multiple volumes on this topic, all we can do here is paint it with very broad strokes.

Beauty surrounds us on a daily basis. It is what pleases the eye, the ear, the skin, the nose, the mouth. A painting, a sculpture, a clay vessel, a weaving may spark an appreciation both for the object and the craftsmanship and lead one friend to experience beauty, for another, it may illicit inspiration or connectivity. The particulars of architecture—such as flying buttresses, stained glass windows, angles of walls and roofs, etc.—not only invite comment and conversation, but become vehicles for deepening a friendship.

Appreciating the beauty of nature—forests, oceans, mountains—can be shared by friends. A mutual hike in the wilderness facilitates a friendship. A day walking on the sandy beach, hearing the waves break onto the shore, and feeling the warm sun on one's skin is a mutual experience of beauty. Mountain climbers remember their experiences of getting to the summit of a peak because the beauty of the trek enhanced their relationship with fellow climbers either in person or later through story telling about the experience.

Likewise, listening to a symphony orchestra, attending a concert, or singing a song together enhances a friendship by appealing to the beauty of music. Sound invites participation. Even the lack of sound, silence, can be an opportunity to nurture beauty. Sometimes friends communicate best without saying a word.

Many of the things that are considered beautiful invite touch. While most works of art are not to be touched, there are those that can be touched, especially in their creation. For example, the potter touches the clay on the wheel, shaping it into the type of vessel desired. The wood carver, appreciating the grain of the block, holds the cedar, oak, or cherry as he or she chisels away everything that is not the image imbedded in the wood.

Maybe the most underused aesthetic aspect is the olfactory. One friend comes to recognize and appreciate the unique scent of the other. This may include the association of a friend with his or her use of a particular cologne or perfume. The aroma of food is a type of beauty that draws together people, along with appreciation for the care required to prepare it. People can savor a chef's presentation of food along with the excellent service of a waiter in a restaurant—both of which enhance the olfactory aspect of the beautiful.

The aesthetic also involves taste. No two people taste something in exactly the same way. One person likes his or her tea sweetened and one does not. One prefers a red sauce to a white one. One friend likes fish; another never thinks of eating it. No matter how tastes differ, one can understand how another appreciates the beauty of taste.

We are not arguing that those relating share exactly the same aesthetics. We are saying that two friends share some common definition of what is beautiful. Beauty inspires a sense of wonder. The beauty of creation—both natural and formed by people—reminds us of the supreme beauty of the Creator. What is named as beautiful, the aesthetic, is a dimension of human wholeness.

Thus what is deemed beautiful encompasses one's whole environment from the wide, open spaces of the outdoors to the inner, candlelit corners of one's room. It also includes the outer beauty of bodily form and the inner beauty of the essence or personality of the other.

Conclusion

Thus, the humanly whole person is one who has integrated, and continues to integrate, all the aspects or dimensions of self, namely, intellectual, psychological, emotional, physical, sexual, spiritual, and aesthetic. We usually do not isolate any one of these aspects, saying to ourselves, "I'm only going to be emotional about my sexual experience." The intellectual, psychological, physical, and aesthetic are present, too, in a sexual experience. Some people will recognize that sex is also a spiritual experience. Others will declare that recreating is both a physical and an aesthetic experience. However, all aspects are intertwined in human wholeness. All aspects function as one to make each person the unique individual he or she is. Through sharing our unique selves with others, we enrich others, and they enrich us.

Questions for Reflection and Discussion

1. In your experience, are there aspects of human wholeness in addition to those presented here?

2. Beside those presented here, what other images can be used to speak about human wholeness? What images do you associate with your experience of human wholeness?

3. What would you add to the definitions of the aspects of human wholeness presented here: intellectual, psychological, emotional, physical, sexual, spiritual, and aesthetic?

4. Do you think there are additional aspects of human wholeness not addressed here? What are they? Explain each.

5. Choose one of your friendships and evaluate it in terms of the aspects of human wholeness: intellectual, psychological, emotional, physical, sexual, spiritual, and aesthetic. What do you discover from your evaluation? With what aspects of human wholeness do you connect within your friendships? How are they experienced?

Chapter 2

Friendship
A Definition

O NCE WE UNDERSTAND THE seven aspects that weave together to form a whole person, we can see that a friendship is based on the degree of connectivity made between two people in some or all of those aspects. We cannot write about adult friendship without defining it. Because the noun *friendship* implies a static reality, the best way to get at the definition of the word is to think of it in terms of a verb: *friendshipping*. With this understanding, we come closer to naming the act or process of two adults relating to each other. Thus, *friendshipping* is a self-motivated process of sharing who one is with another. This cannot occur alone or with some thing, as Buber makes clear in his famous book, *I & Thou:* "I require a You to become; becoming I, I say You. All actual life is encounter."[1] Buber adds, "Persons appear by entering into relation to other persons."[2] Of course, one of the two people must speak the first words or make the first move to establish the friendship, and then the other must reciprocate with a response. In other words, some connectivity must occur in one or several aspects of human

1. Buber, *I & Thou*, 62.
2. Ibid., 112.

wholeness. Then, as two people relate, they both get to know their own selves more as they simultaneously get to know the other.

Thus, a friendship is a dynamic process that begins when one adult acknowledges another as a being endowed with basic human dignity and worthy and able to relate. Indeed, *friendshipping* only becomes possible between two people when each puts the other first. The process of *friendshipping* requires that one person respects the other to the equal or greater degree than he or she respects himself or herself. The process of *friendshipping* requires that both people have a genuine concern for each other's well being. In a friendship, one person meets the other where he or she is and, instead of attempting to change or mold him or her to one's image, one seeks to know and be known, to relate to the other.

Because *friendshipping* is a human process, it is limited by the limitations of the two people involved in it. One person is able to relate to another only to the degree of his or her ability. If the friendship reaches a plateau, both persons may agree to leave it there for a while. But sooner or later it either reconnects or dies. When the friendship potential is exhausted, the relationship will end, as there is nothing more to process. This is why no two experiences of friendship can ever be alike, and it assists in explaining why it is so difficult to classify or subcategorize friendships.

For them to work, friendships require articulated boundaries, which can be changed as the *friendshipping* continues. A boundary is a limit both persons set on the friendship. For example, a business relationship establishes the boundaries that fence out all that does not pertain to the business and fences in all that does. Through vows, a marriage relationship fences out all other sexual partners and fences in only the two people who have promised fidelity to each other.

In *friendshipping*, the desire both to know and to be known by the other person means that each discloses himself or herself and receives the self-disclosure of the other. Self-knowledge comes through *friendshipping*. We gain knowledge of ourselves by giving ourselves away to others with whom we *friendship*.

Indeed, self-knowledge enables each person to be himself or herself. Merton says, "I *am* myself. I do not *make* myself or bring myself into conformity with some nonsensical ideal."[3] What each person seeks is just to be himself or herself, the person God created him or her to be. Each moves toward another out of the security of his or her self-knowledge. Covey calls this a sense of "persistent selfhood."[4] Who one is exists not in reputation, possessions, fame, status, net worth, etc. If it is founded in any one of those, one's life is a constant attempt to protect, to insure one's reputation, properties, position, and securities.

Powell says that "there are three stages to self-knowledge: to know yourself, to be yourself, and to forget yourself."[5] We know ourselves, are ourselves, and forget ourselves through *friendshipping*. Powell says that these are not three separate stages, but that we are engaged in all three as a process. The more we know ourselves, the more we can be ourselves and forget ourselves. The more we can be ourselves, the more we can forget ourselves and know ourselves. And the more we forget ourselves, the more we can know ourselves and are ourselves.

Merton came to this conclusion early in his monastic life. He writes:

> Finally I am coming to the conclusion that my highest ambition is to be what I already am. That I will never fulfill my obligation to surpass myself unless I first accept myself, and if I accept myself fully in the right way, I will have already surpassed myself. For it is the unaccepted self that stands in my way and will come to do so as long as it is not accepted. When it has been accepted—it is my own stepping stone to what is above me. Because this is the way man has been made by God.[6]

In every friendship two people share a unique, one-of-a-kind dynamic which includes responsibility, presence, openness, time,

3. Merton, *Intimate Merton*, 284.
4. Covey, Dai*ly Reflections*, 104.
5. Powell, "Know Thyself," 32.
6. Merton, *Intimate Merton*, 130.

freedom, trust, communication, and sharing of life experiences. This book is written from the perspective of the general U.S. Caucasian culture. What may be true of this part of American culture may not be for other cultures. How people *friendship* is dictated, enhanced, and limited by cultural mores or customs.

Responsibility

A healthy friendship with another person, one that is true *friendshipping*, is only possible if both people are independent, responsible adults. Interdependence is possible only when both adults have achieved independence. This means that both people have taken control of their lives and hold themselves responsible for their decisions, especially that to enter into a relationship with another. The degree of health of a friendship is dependent upon the degree of healthy responsibility assumed by each partner in it.

Presence

Being physically present one to another requires another living person. One person brings himself or herself physically into the sight of another person for the optimum experience of presence. While a degree of presence can be achieved through the use of the telephone and e-mail and other electronic devices, true presence requires one person to be in the physical presence of another. And even though physical presence does not always imply true attentiveness, it is as close as human beings can get to authentic presence.

Presence also implies authenticity, believability, trustworthiness, and reliability. Insofar as one can know who one is, as this is a lifetime process of becoming, he or she presents his or her true self to another. Authenticity makes genuine presence possible. All roles, which can both help us identify who we are and who we are not, are set aside in the effort truly to be who we are genuinely in the presence of the other.

Openness

For a relationship to grow between two people, openness to the other is required. Openness, the ability to receive whatever the other offers, requires honesty on the part of the giver. He or she gives only what is true. Openness also requires genuineness; there can be nothing that is not authentic in both people.

Such openness can be characterized by a spirit of adventure. In *friendshipping*, two people explore each other in openness. Environment affects the degree of openness. Two men may find sharing in physical exercise, outdoor activities, or manual labor more conducive to openness than a seat on a bus. Two women may enjoy the openness that lunch or shopping provides to an office party. And a male-female relationship can find a quiet corner in a restaurant conducive to sharing life experiences that a family gathering can't provide.

Time

Friendshipping requires time. Without time, presence is impossible. And without presence, openness can easily deteriorate. Time refers to taking hours to be with the other, to spend time with the other giving and receiving, to sharing time with the other in activities both enjoy.

People may have to schedule time with each other. Because they are involved in so many things, *friendshipping* requires that both persons schedule time to be in the physical presence of the other.

Freedom

In order for *friendshipping* to occur, both people must be totally and radically free to be themselves, to be free from worry about being manipulated or controlled by the other, to be free to redefine or leave the friendship, to be free not to be possessed by the other or to possess the other. Two individuals enter a relationship and never impose their differences upon each other. Rather, each contains the other's differences in himself or herself and transcends them.

Love can flourish only in freedom. Love sets free the other person in the relationship so that he or she can be who he or she is. Freedom enables one to get out of self, to be other-focused, even as one is getting into the depths of self and revealing who he or she is. Elshtain says, "We cannot offer the gift of self to one another if we ourselves are entirely consumed by consumption."[7] In freedom, love enables the two people in a friendship to keep pushing and pulling back fences that contain the self so that the territory for encounter keeps getting bigger and bigger. The love that frees fosters both persons to move out of the friendship to others and relate to others so as to be able to bring back to, and share with, the friend the fruits of their *friendshipping* outward.

The freedom of one person to enter into a relationship sparks the same freedom in the other to desire the relationship. A healthy friendship fosters the mutual freedom of both persons, and, consequently, enhances their self-knowledge.

True *friendshipping* does not enslave or neutralize individuals. Rather, it super-personalizes them so that they are free to continue to become their distinctive selves.

Trust

A friendship requires radical trust. Both persons promise confidentiality, respect for whom each is and what each reveals about self. Trust enables each to be himself or herself and to share that self with the other without fear of having his or her self-disclosure criticized by the other or disclosed to anyone else. Trust eliminates the basic human fear of getting hurt. And without the quieting or elimination of fear, the process of *friendshipping* cannot even begin.

7. Elshtain, "Families," 20.

Communication

Shea says that relationship is "the offer of cooperation in the midst of competition."[8] And isn't that what communication is—the offer to cooperate with one person when many others are competing for our attention? Attentive and intentional listening to the other enables true dialogue to take place. Covey says that if one person wants to interact effectively with another, he or she first needs to understand the other.[9] We listen not just with our ears, but with our eyes, heart, face, and feelings. Attentive listening implies that we are paying attention to the other's behavior—responses and reactions—and our own as well. As we listen to the other, we assign meaning to what he or she says. Covey calls this "empathetic listening." It "gets inside another person's frame of reference. You look out through it, you see the world the way they see the world, you understand their paradigm, you understand how they feel."[10] He adds, "The essence of empathetic listening is not that you agree with someone; it's that you fully, deeply, understand that person, emotionally as well as intellectually."[11]

In authentic dialogue, two people desire to hear what the other person is saying—not to get him or her to agree or to say what one wants to hear. In authentic dialogue, two people seek to understand each other on their own terms. Covey says, "Integrity means avoiding any communication that is deceptive, full of guile, or beneath the dignity of people."[12] In authentic dialogue, both people can hear the silence between the words the other speaks. Through dialogue, both disclose their strengths and weaknesses and seek the strengths and weaknesses of the other.

Generous listening and dialogue flow from openness. And generous listening and dialogue present the two friends the possibility of change, an opportunity to be more of whom each

8. Shea, *Elijah*, 55.

9. Cf. Covey, *Daily Reflections*, 118.

10. Ibid., 119.

11. Ibid.

12. Ibid., 116.

currently is, and the occasion to accept or help shape a new or beneficial idea.

Sharing Life Experiences

Where there are presence, openness, time, freedom, trust, and communication, both people can share their life experiences. Through their life experiences, they share themselves with each other and their ideas, hopes, dreams, anxieties, fears, successes, joys, and sorrows. There is no experience in which the other does not have an interest, because it may be the very one that assists him or her to understand himself or herself while coming to a deeper knowledge of the other.

Because human beings are mortal, all earthly relationships are impermanent. *Friendshipping* can last only as long as both friends are living. But the beauty of a relationship is that even when both persons agree to end the friendship or when it ends because one person dies, one still retains aspects of the friendship. Who each has become through the relationship up to its end cannot be erased. The impermanence of *friendshipping* does not affect the influence left on both persons by the other through their friendship process.

Every relationship is a dialectic, a process of enrichment and diminishment. When one person receives the presence, openness, time, freedom, trust, communication, and life experiences of another, he or she is enriched. But when he or she gives presence, openness, time, freedom, trust, communication, and shares life experiences with another, he or she is diminished. In *friendshipping* people experience collectively that which is bigger than they are individually. And that is the transcendent quality of friendship; it is always in process, and continually fosters self-definition, self-knowledge, and greater revelation of God.

Questions for Reflection and Discussion

1. In addition to what you read here, how do you define friendship? How do you define relationship? How are the two definitions connected?

2. What categories of friendship have you nurtured in your relationships?

3. Why is self knowledge so important in a friendship? If there is no self knowledge on the part of one or both parties in a friendship, what might the consequences be?

4. What qualities do you think are necessary for a healthy friendship?

5. How has the impermanence of friendships affected your investment in them? What losses have you experienced in your life that may have contributed to this?

Chapter 3

Transcendence
through Relationship

A FRIENDSHIP IS GREATER than the two people involved in it. A friendship is evidence of a yearning for what is deep and profound in our human experience, in our hunger for meaning. This experience is called transcendence; momentarily, it takes us beyond our human limitations. People often speak of standing beside themselves. We are able to be self-conscious and other-conscious while also being self-evaluative. We discover a tension between our subjective and objective selves which makes us aware, from a Judeo-Christian point of view, that the greater-than-the-two-of-us is nothing other than the presence of God mediated by the presence of one person to another.

Beginning with the understanding that the human person is created in the image and likeness of God and that each human person is the clearest reflection of one of the myriad possibilities of God, we understand that in friendship God is disclosed to God. The God who breathed the breath of life into people so that they became living beings (cf. Gen 2:7) continues to breathe the breath of life into us so that we, too, become living beings. Thus the image of God, who is one person, meets the image of God, who is the other, and the Divine is experienced through the human relating of two people. Merton writes that God "can be known in Himself only by His own revelation of Himself"[1] through people created in God's image.

Each person flashes forth some aspect of the divine presence. Commonly called the *imago Dei*, the spark of God's life in each person is the orientation of a human being toward union with God. If we are, to some degree like God, we can aspire to know the Divine, to whom we are inevitably drawn nearer and nearer as our final end through our friendship.

Elshtain says: "Our self-awareness is both an achievement and a gift. Indeed, it is the *communion* of persons that is the authentic *imago Dei*."[2] Then, she adds: "Communion expresses more than help or helper; it names the existence of the person *for* another; of the gift of the self to another. It is a special reciprocity; it affords intimations of divine communion."[3]

Merton addresses this directly, writing, "To belong to God I have to belong to myself. . . . None of me belongs to anybody but God. . . . I love everybody and am possessed by nobody, not held, not bound."[4] He also says that "there is a sense in which my own deepest self is in God and even expresses Him as 'word.'"[5] Merton cautions that we must get rid "of the self that blocks the view of truth."[6] Instead of viewing ourselves as outside of or distinct from God, we see that we are in God. God is the connection between everyone. In the process of relating we go beyond our individuality into the common realm where we are connected to everyone through God.

The human beingness, that basic quality which makes a person a human being (some call this "soul" or "personhood"), touches the human beingness of another and a divine connection

1. Merton, *Intimate Merton*, 115.
2. Elshtain, "Families," 20.
3. Ibid.
4. Merton, *Intimate Merton*, 75.
5. Ibid., 180.
6. Ibid., 193.

is established between the two people. As a human being, each of us is aware of himself or herself as a person existing in the world. Being human is being able to experience transcendence because humans are able to reflect on themselves and their experiences, to be conscious of themselves in the world and in God, to some degree.

Because all of being, existence, the essence of God, is intricately interrelated and inseparable, the ability to experience transcendence comes from the Creator. It is the way God formed people to be—in God. The psalmist asks God, "Where can I go from your spirit? Or where can I flee from your presence?" (Ps 139:7) People who seek wholeness want to experience the fullness of whom they were created to be, and this can be accomplished best through relating with another human being through whom God is revealed. Haughey says that mature love "develops a bond between God and the person that is rightly akin to the friendship between two human beings."[7]

This process of coming to wholeness, integration, lasts a lifetime. As such, a person's experiences of intimate human friendships form a narrative of life. This narrative is woven together from all previous and current relationships. This beginning point of our shared human existence prompts us to understand not only the relationship disclosing it, but the God who enables human persons to experience it. In other words, the experience of a friendship that springs from the depths of us and desires to be expressed is nothing other than the ground of existence, pure being, which enables each person both to relate to others and to probe the depths of their relationships with them.

Two persons' experience of being greater than the relationship they have entered into is transcendence, the opportunity to share the Divine with each other and with God simultaneously. One human mediates God to another. Thus, any common human experience of relating, because it is grounded in being or God, can be the beginning point for understanding one's lifetime narrative of friendships.

7. Haughey, "Pneumatology," 34.

St. Paul reminds us of the dialectic involved in both human-human and God-human relationships when he writes that now we can "know only in part, . . . but when the complete comes, the partial will come to an end. Now I know only in part; then I will know fully, even as I have been fully known" (1 Cor 13:12–13). The experience of transcendence is like knowing and being known, like being known inside-in and then being known inside-out.

Another metaphor for transcendence is vision. In a relationship each person has a vision of who he or she is, who God is, and how the world works. When those visions are shared, understood, or grasped by each other, some of God's vision for people is also perceived. God wraps people in God's vision and people gradually make it their own.

Transcendence is like transparency; both people are able to see through each other, while also seeing through themselves. And in the light that both flashes out and penetrates in, the divine is illuminated. Merton refers to this as "a complete and holy transparency: living, praying, and writing in the light of the Holy Spirit, losing [oneself] entirely by becoming public property just as Jesus is public property . . . ."[8]

In this regard, the synoptic gospels portray transcendence as transfiguration. Jesus appears to his disciples Peter, James, and John on a mountain with Moses and Elijah in dazzling white clothes (cf. Mark 9:28). The triple sets of three people (Peter, James, John), three prophets (Jesus, Moses, Elijah), and Peter's offer to erect three dwellings denotes a great theophany, a manifestation of God as light. A relationship of two people in God is a theophany which occurs through each person's transparency.

Thus, human friendships are always spiritual experiences, even though those involved in them may not always be conscious that they are. Once we have experienced transcendence, we realize that our definition of living is not what we thought it was. Living is not reaching a plateau and staying there, like Peter wanted to stay on the mountain with Jesus. Living is the process of becoming, always being in the process of becoming who each person is, who

8. Merton, *Intimate Merton*, 73.

we are in relationship. We cannot go back to what we once were, as a bridge between one person and another has been built and the bridge itself is being, God.

In transcendence two people experience themselves as existing both with and beyond limits. They are spirits in the world. Their desire to know each other is infinite; it always exceeds their grasp of the known. By focusing their desire to know on their relationship, they come to know not only the other person in intimacy, but also God. Teasdale says, "The self-awareness I have of myself as self-aware is the vehicle through which the divine can communicate with me."[9]

Therefore, transcendence offers one in relationship the ability to be saying in his or her head what the other is putting into words with his or her lips. Transcendence offers the fulfillment of experiencing human love, a metaphor for divine love, which is more encompassing than the friendship. The Song of Solomon describes transcendent love: Love is "a raging flame," like the very flame of the LORD (8:6).The First Letter of John makes this clear when the author exhorts his readers: "Beloved, let us love one another, because love is from God; everyone who loves is born of God and knows God. Whoever does not love does not know God, for God is love" (4:7–8).

Ludwig says that "in the mystery of human existence which knows itself as unexplainable, we discover the human as 'finite infinity,' and 'indefinability that is conscious of itself,' the very embodiment of the mystery we call God."[10] Through intimate personal relationships, each individual experiences transcendence and experiences himself or herself as a whole person, yet also part of a unified whole, in God. Through friendship, we recognize that we are designed by God to be more than who we experience ourselves to be. As spiritual beings in a relationship, which is itself spiritual, both persons possess from the beginning an orientation towards God in whom they "live and move and have [their] being" (Acts 17:28). Their relationship with each other creates a desire for

9. Teasdale, *Mystic Heart*, 100.

10. Ludwig, *Grace*, 106.

a deeper relationship with God, which creates a deeper desire for a relationship with each other, which creates a desire for a deeper relationship with God, etc.

Thus, as the love shared by two people in a relationship keeps growing, so does their self-knowledge and knowledge of the other. They delve deeper and deeper into the mystery that each is and touch the Divine. God is found at the core of the existence of every human person. The deep mutual respect that flows from this awareness enables each person to reach out and embrace all the extremes and differences of the others and hold them within himself or herself without confusion. The extremes and differences in each individual are the unique fingerprints of the Creator.

Therefore, by knowing himself or herself, a person makes contact with God. Metaphorically, touching another person and permitting him or her to touch in return, one touches God through contact with another's being. At that moment, the door opens to an experience of God who shares who the Holy One is through our human relationships. The presence of one person to another makes both aware of God disclosing who the Holy One is to the two people in their being (cf. Matt 18:20).

Transcendence involves an exchange of grace, the process of God sharing who the Holy One is with people. Grace, then, is the very movement between one person and another. God shares who God is, grace, with each. Thus, grace is *relationshipping* between God and each person, God's self-communication. Buber says, "The You encounters me by grace—it cannot be found by seeking."[11] When two people share God's grace with each other, they complete the circle of grace: Grace is a gift freely given, received, and given away, like the grace initiator—God. Huebsch says, "Grace can only be shared, only shared in love, in the context of a loving friendship."[12] Sharing grace is as close as two people can come to being like God, to experience transcendence. That's why Paul says "not to accept the grace of God in vain" (2 Cor 6:1).

11. Buber, *I & Thou*, 62.

12. Huebsch, *New Look*, 133.

The experience of transcendence serves as a catalyst for growth in both the human-human relationship and the Divine-human relationship. God draws people into a relationship just as one person invites another into a friendship. Shared grace never satisfies; one always wants more. The result is growth in the human relationship.

Questions for Reflection and Discussion

1. What do you understand transcendence to be in a friendship? How have you experienced this?

2. In what ways are you continuing to grow in self-awareness?

3. In what ways have you experienced human wholeness as a lifetime process?

4. What is transparency in a friendship? How have you experienced this?

5. How is grace shared through a friendship? How have you experienced this?

Chapter 4

The Dialectic of Enrichment and Diminishment in Relationship

INITIATING A RELATIONSHIP WITH another begins ordinarily with significant caution, as self-consciousness seems to prohibit one person from at first sharing more than what is peripheral to human beingness. In other words, only the superficial is revealed, such as occupation, place of residence, interests, accomplishments. Sometimes a relationship is begun because of a common interest in sports, reading, movies, etc. The initial invitation to friendship may be the attraction of one person to the beauty, skill, interest, etc. of another. Whatever draws two people together can lead to an intentional or conscious relationship. Even though we know that there is a desire for transcendence within us that seeks expression and union, we are reticent to be totally open in the beginning.

Once the first move is made and the other accepts the invitation, two begin to enter into deeper levels of sharing. This does not come automatically or immediately, but very cautiously. The degree that one person reveals human beingness corresponds to the degree that the other does the same, and vice-versa. Together they form a dialectic, a dialogue that leads to further exploration. Depending upon the two persons involved in the relationship, this process continues over days, months, and years.

Each time two people re-encounter each other they move quickly through the various levels of human beingness they have already probed together and, gradually, achieve authenticity, that state where each is totally who he or she is. Intimacy in the form of close familiarity is developed. Two people connect more deeply through the aspects of human wholeness. There is less and less that is not shared by the two people in the friendship. The relationship continues to delve into intimacy and greater depths of authenticity as long as both parties continue to support and, simultaneously, challenge the other to be who he or she is becoming.

Intimacy involves the dialectic of enrichment and diminishment, expansion and depletion. Enrichment comes from what is shared with the other. Indeed, according to Elshtain, "the Christian gift economy holds that in giving we are enriched."[1] Each person is enriched by another person in a relationship by the clarifications the other person helps make about self, by what each learns about personality through the help of the other, through the other's challenge when he or she detects that one is not being honest with self or him or her.

Two people are diminished even as they are enriched, because they must remove some self in order to have more self. Diminishment comes as one risks sharing in intimacy who he or she is with another, as one gives up some of self (ego) in order to have some of the other's, as one helps the other person achieve identity and honesty with himself or herself and he or she does the same with the other.

This simultaneous enrichment and diminishment, expansion and depletion, is often referred to as synergy between two people. It's an energy which passes between them, like electricity between two cars hooked up with battery cables. Both are simultaneously jump-started, but both also are simultaneously drained. It is this dialectic of relationship which makes the relationship both risky

1. Elshtain, "Families," 20.

and exciting. It presupposes two free, responsible, and vulnerable people who decide to relate to each other on a level upon which both are comfortable.

According to Elshtain, ". . . The self emerges only through a project of reciprocity that includes expectations; that, indeed, we only actually hold to love given when we give love back because love is a work of dignity and recognition."[2] Haughy states, "Love given and love received makes two one. . . . Therefore, by the Holy Spirit not only is God in us, but we are also in God."[3] Likewise, in John's Gospel, Jesus tells his disciples to abide in him as he abides in them (cf. 15:4).

Before either inviting another person into a relationship or accepting the invitation from another to enter into one, a person must know who he or she is, so that he or she can be humanly authentic, all that he or she was created to be. By knowing self, one knows the God who created him or her. This God is not outside of a person, but is living within him or her, identified with his or her innermost being.

In a way of speaking, God has left God's fingerprints on each person and signed each as a one-of-a-kind object of art. As such, each individual represents one of the myriad possibilities of God's revelation of who God is. Every human being is an icon or a representative symbol of the divine, who, dialectically, comes to know who God is through relating with those created in the Holy One's image.

Just as one person offers the invitation to enter into a relationship, God does the same. God initiates relationships with human beings. In some sense it is true to say that God seeks God's self, since each human person is already connected to the Holy One by the fact of his or her being or spirit. This being is a gift from God, a grace that is intrinsic to being human.

Through the gift of creation, God fills all with grace and spirit, which people share with each other. Just as one person can only give himself or herself to another person in his or her capacity to

2. Ibid., 22.

3. Haughey, "Pneumatology," 34.

receive, so God can only give God to one who has the capacity to receive God—human beings. In other words, God creates people not only for intimacy with each other, but also for intimacy with God. James tells his readers, "Draw near to God, and he will draw near to you" (4:8).

Thus, just as one person makes offers to others to enter into personal relationships throughout life, so God makes the offer of grace present throughout the whole of life. And just as one can never be one hundred percent sure where he or she is in relating with another person, one can never be sure exactly where one is in relating to God, although God is always pursuing a relationship. As in any relationship process, the degree or intensity differs from time to time.

Both people in an intimate relationship offer to surround the other in love, to make his or her self-discovery and self-revelation take place in an atmosphere of trust which is fostered by love. God does the same. Just as one person invites and, then, loves another into a relationship of trust, God makes the first move by creating people with a capacity for God and, then, loving them and inviting them to the freedom of transcendence which exists only in total trust and vulnerability.

Responding to God's offer, a person suddenly discovers that more grace has been given as quickly as one made a response. Shea says, "There is more love when it is given away than when it is kept, more love for those who receive it."[4] Simultaneously, one is also further freed to be who he or she is and to continue the discovery of whom he or she is, a process that lasts a lifetime—and maybe even beyond.

Human freedom is a prerequisite for any relationship. One cannot relate to another in fear. One cannot relate to another who forces a relationship upon him or her. This is also true of one's relationship with God. Like in human relationships in which once the initial move is made, the initiator waits to see if he or she gets any response, God does the same. Even Jesus declares, "I am standing at the door knocking; if you hear my voice and open the door,

4. Shea, "Eucharist," 15.

I will come into you . . . (Rev. 3:20).While the offer of God's self-communication is directed towards knowledge and freedom, its purpose is to enable one to enter into immediate knowledge and love of God and find salvation. The event of a relationship cannot be completed unless it is freely accepted by the one to whom it is offered.

The Holy One does not force God's self upon anyone. Just like others accept or reject an offer of a relationship, so do we have the freedom to accept or reject God's offer. Just like upon acceptance of an offer, we enter into a deeper level of sharing and transcendence with another person, so once we accept God's offer we open ourselves to the Creator and the gift of grace is complete. In the presence of the other we recognize the presence of God.

Just like two people in a relationship free each other to be totally who the other is and to revel in such freedom, the Holy One does the same in God-human relationships. As two human beings experience growing together as a simultaneous growing apart (as we come to know who we are, we also come to know who we are not), God in relationship to humans and humans in relationship to God experience the same in each other's presence. Like one is a vessel waiting to be filled with the grace of the relationship of another, so is one a vessel already and waiting to be filled with God's own life.

Each person is always in the process of becoming who he or she is through his or her intimate human relationships. Likewise, each person is always in the process of becoming who he or she is through his or her relationship with God. Because each experiences the process of both his or her becoming and the other person's becoming through relating, both people experience revelation through their relationship and their simultaneous relationship with the Holy One.

The difference in one's individual relationship with God is that the Holy One had to make the first move and make one capable of receiving God's grace. Once one responds to God's offer, he or she is transformed by the grace which remains freely given.

What is important to keep in mind is the tension that the dialectic creates. One is becoming who he or she is, and yet one never reaches total potential. One is free, and yet one is always becoming freer. Tension must be kept in place in order to achieve human wholeness.

This does not mean to imply that one always chooses grace. In human relationships, one often chooses not to respond to the other. One may hurt the other through what he or she says or doesn't say, through what action he or she takes or doesn't take, through what gift he or she offers or doesn't bring. This means that a person chooses to go it alone or chooses separation or selfishness. In one's relationship with God, as a human being, one experiences the same limitations and the fact that he or she is not God. In other words, each person has the ability to sin. Like a person can with people, he or she can reject God, although in doing so, one also rejects his or her source of fulfillment.

This dynamism which can draw a person away from the realization of that which is always present as an offer and makes real the possibility of rejecting the only reality which will fulfill and complete one, God's self-communicating love, is original sin. We are born into this human condition and experience it as neverending. It is the price of self-awareness, which is marked by the tension of being an individual who has the freedom to choose.

A consequence of freedom in a human relationship is that one can choose not to initiate a relationship or to reject the invitation of relationship from another. One may also choose to end a relationship. A consequence of one's freedom in relating with God is his or her ability to reject the Holy One's offer of relationship.

What a person does with his or her freedom in a human relationship depends on who he or she is and who he or she is becoming. Likewise, what one does with his or her freedom in his or her relationship with God depends on who he or she is and who he or she is becoming.

Thus, sin may be understood as the failure either to respond initially to God's offer of a relationship or to continue to respond to God's offer of a relationship. Basically, one decides that he or she can become who he or she is without God and without others. It's going it alone. And while God doesn't stop one from going it alone, our perception is that the Holy One doesn't recommend that one take such a road. Security and safety are found in a relationship with another, just like security and safety are found in relationship with God. That security is not the warm, cozy feeling that is often associated with the word "safety," but it is a secure freedom to continue to explore or probe the mystery of the other and the mystery of the Other, knowing that both put us in contact with the divinity we are and we are becoming. God became human in the person of Jesus to show humans how to enter into relationship with the Divine.

While one may stray from an intimate human relationship, he or she is drawn by the more powerful force of the essence of the relationship between himself or herself and the other and between himself or herself and God. We can never be totally out of grace because we're always being loved by God, even when we don't think we are loveable. And just as the other will, we hope, forgive us for digression, so does God forgive us when we stray. One can forgive the other from the depths of who he or she is, like God forgives from within the depths of who God is.

Questions for Reflection and Discussion

1. What do you understand the dialectic of enrichment and diminishment to be in a friendship? Explain.

2. How has one of your human friendships revealed God's offer of a divine friendship to you?

3. What conditions must be fulfilled for a human friendship to flourish? What conditions must be fulfilled for a divine friendship to flourish?

4. Explain the dialectic of initiation and response. Apply it to one of your friendships. What do you discover? Apply it to your friendship with God. What do you discover?

5. What is the role of freedom in a friendship? Which of your friendships frees you the most? How?

6. Are there aspects of your self that lack wholeness and authenticity? How does this affect you and your relationships?

7. Where are you in the continual process of becoming whole? Do your relationships and friendships support this process?

Chapter 5

Jesus

Paradigm of Human Wholeness through Relationship

Relationship with God

JESUS IS A PARADIGM of who human beings are to be. He is the model for a healthy and whole relationship between God and people and between one person and another. As a human being, he called God "Abba" (Mark 14:36), translated as daddy or father, indicating the intimacy between them. What sets Jesus apart from the rest of us is the complete faithfulness to his relationship with God. While we often stumble and fall, hurting the one we love, Jesus never did. He remained faithful to his relationship with God to death.

In the person of Jesus, the eternal Word of God became flesh, human, and demonstrated what being human means—cooperating with God. He accepted God's grace, God's offer of relationship. Through his relationship with God, Jesus reveals that every human being achieves self-understanding or self-knowledge through relating with God and others which facilitates the reciprocity of grace.

Jesus represents the culmination of God's plan to unite heaven and earth. While we can never begin to understand this plan adequately, Jesus becomes "the image . . . of a perfected human person,"[1] the example of how grace triumphs even through death. He kept his focus on the grace he and God shared, and he cooperated with it, even when tempted not to.

In Jesus, "the human expresses the divine."[2] O'Grady emphasizes, "God chose as revelation the human form, the man Jesus" in whom "the human becomes the localization of the divine."[3] Jesus is "the human face of God."[4] Thus, "the human and the divine are not disparate or separated, but are united in one historical person,"[5] who "lived what he believed in an integral way," and "knew his God, knew his mission, and lived accordingly."[6]

The union of the human and divine in Jesus is analogous to the *friendshipping* that takes place between two people. Ludwig says,

> Just as their union does not subvert their freedom or suppress their individuality but, in fact, calls forth and enhances both freedom and individuality, so too in this union, the dynamic orientation of human nature towards God is realized in the free response which accepts God's offer unhesitatingly.[7]

Furthermore,

> Jesus' humanity is in no way diminished, but rather fulfilled and completed through his relationship with God. His human reality in its radical union with God accomplished through the surrender of himself to the mystery of God, is the uniquely perfect fulfillment of human being. In him, the authentically human and the divine

1. O'Grady, *Models*, 11.

2. Ibid., 37.

3. Ibid.

4. Ibid., 38.

5. Ibid., 39.

6. Ibid., 41.

7. Ludwig, *Grace*, 147.

are not opposed or in competition, but are distinctively themselves precisely in their relation to each other.[8]

Jesus is a paradigm for those who relate because, like them, he was "called by God to embody God's very life and love in the world."[9] Two people in a relationship develop signs and symbols that illustrate their uniqueness and knowing of each other; such signs and symbols represent both the individual and the relationship. "[S]o analogously does God express God himself through embodiment in Jesus."[10] Jesus, "this becoming of God in the Word Incarnate, is the decisive manifestation of God's will to share God's divine life with all humanity."[11]

When we love the other in a friendship, we offer the other a share in the divine stream of grace that courses through us from our individual relationship with God. When we accept the offer from another, we receive a share in the divine stream of grace that courses through the other's relationship with God. Human being, which is divine being, contacts human being and God. Thus, according to Ludwig,

> There can be no real or existential distinction between the divine and the human: To love God is to love our brothers and sisters; indeed, our situation is such that we become the embodiment of God's self-gift to them and they to us. God loves others through us; God loves us through others.[12]

Through relationship love we are most like God and best able to experience the depth of love's freeing power.

According to O'Grady, "The closer a person is to God, the more freedom that person experiences."[13] Therefore, "Jesus, the

8. Ibid.
9. Ibid., 148.
10. Ibid.
11. Ibid.
12. Ibid.
13. O'Grady, *Models*, 42.

graced man, lived in freedom and in harmony"[14] and becomes the paradigm not only for one's personal relationship with God, but for human relationships as well. As O'Grady so eloquently puts it, "Jesus fulfilled his human destiny. He lived for God and all who met him knew it."[15]

Shea states that Jesus received "life at every moment from the divine source, and he acknowledged this mystic flow."[16] O'Grady adds that Jesus "founded his life on his self-awareness and his sense of God"[17] which is what those do who *relationship*. While we cannot reach the level of wholeness Jesus reached, he is the model for what we seek. His life "gives the elements that will make up the content of the human in its highest form. If the divine can be expressed to human beings only in a human way, then the highest example of the human spirit can alone be the vehicle that God uses to reveal himself."[18]

Jesus possessed a unique relationship of Son to Father and "that is what makes him distinctive and gives him his identity"[19] and makes him a paradigm for all who *relationship*. Thus, "in every person there is the potential for manifesting the presence of the divine. Jesus reminded us of this."[20] Likewise,

> The human face of God revealed in Jesus allows the possibility of many other expressions in other human faces. Everyone has the spark of the divine that the coming of Jesus has recalled. . . . Jesus revealed the presence of God in himself, but also reminded all people of their potential to reveal the divine.[21]

14. Ibid.
15. Ibid.
16. Shea, "Eucharist," 15.
17. O'Grady, *Models*, 42.
18. Ibid., 42-43.
19. Ibid., 48.
20. Ibid., 50.
21. Ibid.

"If Jesus is the human face of God, and if every human person can display the divine, then God is present in every person—there is a[n] *enhypostatis* that is part of human experience."[22] In other words, in every person there is a merging of the Divine and the human.

This is how Jesus becomes a paradigm for human beings: The way to be human is to be divine, and the way to be divine is to be human. "Jesus makes present the divine without ever abandoning our own finite existence."[23] As long as we keep in dialectic the human and divine, we will not go astray. Over-emphasize one, and we can become either completely narcissistically human or narcissistically divine. Jesus demonstrates that "the offer of grace is also and simultaneously the gift of our humanity; we are driven to accept that gift, but we are also afraid of it, partially wanting to reject it."[24] Or as Dyer says, "If we over stress transcendence or otherness, God ceases to have any effective place in our lives. If we overemphasize closeness, we may believe we can manipulate God."[25]

In any authentic relationship, two people can experience God. Their choice to accept each other's gift of grace is simultaneously a choice to accept God's gift of grace. "Grace is loose in the world."[26] It "is all around us; it is easy to get, and it is available to everyone."[27] Relationship is "the direct experience of the saving power of God."[28] Turning toward another person in friendship gives each a glimpse of what turning to God is like. *Friendshipping* happens "when we are in such circumstance that we truly see love, love as the deep structure of life."[29]

Sharing God's grace and love brings us to recognize that reconciliation occurs through human friendship, accepting and being

22. Ibid., 53.
23. Ibid., 52.
24. Ludwig, *Grace*, 155.
25. Dyer, "What Happens at Mass," 28.
26. Ludwig, *Grace*, 167.
27. Heubsch, *New Look*, 112.
28. Ludwig, *Grace*, 157.
29. Ibid., 159.

in relationship with self, others, and God. God is already active in another person's life, just like the Holy One is active in our lives, and the most we can do is to make the other aware of it. Just as God's grace finds each of us, so we find another and through relationships help the other to realize that grace has found him or her.

The Human Dimensions of Jesus' Wholeness

Jesus, the human face of God, serves as a model of how we relate As he is portrayed in the gospels, Jesus connects to God and others through the same dimensions of human wholeness that we do— the intellectual, the psychological, the emotional, the physical, the sexual, the spiritual, and the aesthetic. We limit our demonstration to a few examples from the oldest of the gospels, Mark's.

The intellectual aspect of human wholeness comprises the cognitive facet. It represents the need to study, to learn, to read, to reflect, to discuss, and to meditate on challenging ideas, and enhance or alter previously held concepts. The Markan Jesus demonstrates his intellectual ability by challenging the sabbath law prohibiting work. He and his disciples engage in work by plucking heads of grain. When the Pharisees object, Jesus declares, "The sabbath was made for humankind, and not humankind for the sabbath" (Mark 2:27).

Later in the story, a Syrophoenician woman begs Jesus to heal her daughter. He tells her that "it is not fair to take the children's food and throw it to the dogs" (Mark 7:27). In other words, Jesus refuses to help her because he would be assisting a Gentile before his own people. But the woman proves to be an equal intellectual match for the man from Nazareth. She bests him, stating, ". . . Even the dogs under the table eat the children's crumbs" (Mark 7:28).

The Markan Jesus is also smart enough not to get caught in the trap set for him by his opponents. When the Pharisees come asking for a sign, he tells them that no sign will be given (cf. Mark 8:11–12). Then, after making clear his position, he leaves them standing with their trap sprung.

In the temple in Jerusalem, religious officials find Jesus and ask him to indicate from where he gets his authority, since in the ancient world one got his authority to teach from the man who taught him. Again, Jesus recognizes their trap and poses a question to them. They dare not answer Jesus' question, because either answer they give will indict them. So, once again, Jesus wins the debate with silence (cf. Mark 11:27–33).

The psychological dimension of a person includes the ability to see oneself in the perspective of the long-range plan of one's life and be in the process of implementing it, including the ability to sacrifice what one immediately desires for a greater, future desire. We connect through others through the self-image that each of us shares, even as it is always in the process of development.

The Markan Jesus demonstrates the psychological aspect of human wholeness when he proclaims to those sitting around him inside a house that they are his true relatives, while the members of his family stand outside and are unable to enter. Only Mark tells the reader that Jesus' family thought he was out of his mind (cf. Mark 3:21, 31–35). Jesus presents himself as he is—not as they wish he would be—to those who will listen to him.

Three times he demonstrates that he sees his life as part of God's long-range plan by predicting his suffering, death, and resurrection (cf. Mark 8:31, 9:30, 10:32). Every time he tells his followers about what will take place, they rebuke him, fail to understand what he means, or are afraid to ask him about it.

The Markan Jesus is self-secure enough to venture outside himself. His opening message proclaims an altered world view: "The time is fulfilled, and the kingdom of God has come near; repent, and believe in the good news" (Mark 1:15). He calls fishermen to follow him and they respond (cf. Mark 1:16–20). He does not fear that which represents oppression because he is psychologically free from what others presume bind them. So, before cleansing the Temple (cf. Mark 11:15–19), he curses the fig tree (cf. Mark 11:12–14, 20–25), Israel's sign of prosperity, thus declaring the Temple, the dwelling place of God's presence, null and void. Thus, Jesus demonstrates how a self-differentiated person lives.

Jesus demonstrates psychological wholeness by pointing out the hypocrisy of the scribes, "who like to walk around in long robes, and to be greeted with respect in the marketplaces, and to have the best seats in the synagogues and places of honor at banquets" (Mark 12:38–39). However, "they devour widows' houses and for the sake of appearance say long prayers" (Mark 12:40). From his world view of authenticity, Jesus critiques the inauthenticity of Jewish leaders.

The Markan Jesus is a man of emotion. In both accounts of Jesus feeding thousands of people, the author of Mark's Gospel records that Jesus had compassion for the crowd (cf. Mark 6:30–44; 8:1–10). Moved with pity for a leper, Jesus heals him (cf. Mark 1:40–45), and moved by Bartimeaus' request for mercy, Jesus cures his blindness (cf. Mark 10:46–52). Jesus loves the rich man, whom he tells to sell what he owns, give the money to the poor, and to follow him (cf. Mark 10:17–22).

Before his death, Jesus "began to be distressed and agitated" in Gethsemane, telling his followers, "I am deeply grieved, even to death; remain here, and keep awake" (Mark 14:33–34). Then, after his arrest, he experiences abandonment as all his followers "deserted him and fled" (Mark 14:50). Even though he had told Peter that he would deny him (cf. Mark 14:26–31), he experiences the results of Peter's three-fold "I don't know him" (Mark 14:66–72) and dies declaring that he thinks God has abandoned him: "My God, my God, why have you forsaken me?" (Mark 15:34) Throughout his life, emotions motivate Jesus' ministry to the forgotten, the outcast, the sinners of his world.

Jesus does not hesitate to display the physical dimension of human wholeness, especially through touch. When he reaches out his hand and touches a leper (cf. Mark 1:40–45), he incurs not only the social stigma of quarantine, but the ritual impurity associated with disease by first-century people. The physicality Jesus displays toward a blind man not only leads to Jesus laying his hands on him, but he also puts saliva on his eyes and lays his hands on his eyes to restore his sight (cf. Mark 8:22–26).

The Markan Jesus does not fear the touch of others. Indeed, he permits and praises the woman who enters the all-male gathering in the house of Simon the leper and proceeds to pour out all the costly ointment in an alabaster jar on Jesus' head, declaring that a woman has anointed the Anointed One and prepared his body beforehand for burial (cf. Mark 14:3–9). Earlier in the gospel he permits a woman with hemorrhages to touch his clothes. In so doing he willingly incurs the ritual impurity associated with blood and women during their menstrual cycle (cf. Mark 5:24–34).

His human need for food leads Jesus to eat with tax collectors and sinners (cf. Mark 2:15–17), as well Simon the leper (cf. Mark 14:3–9), and his last meal with his followers (cf. Mark 14:12–25). It is through physical food that his disciples recognize that Jesus is more than his physical body, which he gives to them as food and drink. Some of them had already experienced his transfiguration, his crossing over the boundary of death to life on the other side of the grave to meet with Moses and Elijah (cf. Mark 9:2–8).

Because he is human, Jesus also needs physical rest. He invites his apostles to join him in a deserted place all by themselves to rest a while. Mark tells us that because of the crowds they had no leisure even to eat. So, they get into a boat to a deserted place to rest (cf. Mark 6:30–32).

Jesus fully understood the sexual dimension within the context of his time and place in the world. He taught that the union of man and woman in marriage is what God intended from the time that the Holy One had created the two genders. The two enter into so close a union with each other that they become one flesh and should not be separated by divorce (cf Mark 10:2–9). Two become one while remaining two. Love makes two one, but love also enhances the personal identity of both beloveds.

The Markan Jesus also declares that male and female are equal, quite a radical move in the first century CE. Employing the honor-shame code—a man is always honored and a woman is always shamed—Jesus declares that a man who divorces his wife and marries another woman is guilty of adultery. A man couldn't be accused of adultery because that would imply shaming him; only women were guilty of that sin. Thus, men are brought to the same level as women.

But there is more. The Markan Jesus also declares that if a woman divorces her husband and marries another man, she commits adultery. A woman could not divorce her husband; only he could divorce her. But by stating this, Jesus raises woman to the same level as man. Thus with two sentences, Jesus declares both genders equal (cf. Mark 10:10–12).

In Matthew's Gospel, we find Jesus unraveling the traditional Jewish teaching that a man should always marry. The Matthean Jesus addresses that gender issue by accepting his disciples' insight that it may be better not to marry (cf. Matt 19:10). Chaste or unexpressed sexual energy can be a source of an experience of God taught Aelred of Rievaulx. Then, elevating even those who are eunuchs, those considered sterile or neutered, with the rest of men and women, Jesus states, ". . . There are eunuchs who have been so from birth, and there are eunuchs who have been made eunuchs by others, and there are eunuchs who have made themselves eunuchs for the sake of the kingdom of heaven" (Matt 19:12). Gender, according to Jesus, is to be respected both when it doesn't lead to sexual union and when it does.

The spiritual dimension of human wholeness is displayed by the Markan Jesus when he withdraws from the crowds to pray. He goes up a mountain to pray (cf. Mark 6:46), and in Gethsemane he throws himself on the ground and prays, "Abba, Father, for you all things are possible; remove this cup from me; yet, not what I want, but what you want" (Mark 14:36). He tells his disciples, ". . . Whatever you ask for in prayer, believe that you have received it, and it will be yours" (Mark 11:24), and he exhorts them, "Keep awake and pray that you may not come into the time of trial" (Mark 14:38). Ludwig states that "a life of transcendence requires times of solitude and silence, times away from the noise and the crowds to be with the one we love".[30] So Jesus demonstrated the same in his life, taking time to be with Abba in order to develop their relationship and teaching us the importance of doing the same.

30. Ibid., 164.

The Markan Jesus advocates the giving away of everything in order to follow him sincerely. He tells a crowd and his disciples, "If any want to become my followers, let them deny themselves and take up their cross and follow me" (Mark 8:34). Later, he tells his disciples, who had been arguing about who was greatest, "Whoever wants to be first must be last of all and servant of all" (Mark 9:35). Jesus tells the rich man to sell all he owns and give the money to the poor and follow him (cf. Mark 10:21). And when James and John request the second and third levels of command, Jesus declares, ". . . Whoever wishes to become great among you must be your servant, and whoever wishes to be first among you must be slave of all" (Mark 10:43–44).

The spiritual need to be empty of self, power, money, and greatness in order to be open to God reaches a crescendo in Mark's Gospel with the story about the poor widow who came and put two small copper coins, worth about a penny, in the temple treasury. In the first-century world, the woman was already powerless because she had no man to take care of her. She makes herself even more powerless by giving away her last cent. Jesus tells his disciples, ". . . This poor widow has put in more than all those who are contributing to the treasury. For all of them have contributed out of their abundance; but she out of her poverty has put in everything she had, all she had to live on" (Mark 12:43–44).

The Markan Jesus has a great appreciation for what is beautiful, especially physical human wholeness. Mark's Gospel is peppered with accounts of Jesus' healing mission. He cleanses a leper (cf. 1:40–45), restores a paralytic (cf. 2:1–12), recreates a withered hand (cf. 3:1–6), brings back to life a little girl and a stops a woman's flow of blood (cf. 5:21–43), opens the ears of a deaf man (cf. 7:31–17) and gives back sight to the blind (cf. 8:22–26; 10:46–52).

Jesus appreciates the wilderness. He goes there to be tempted (cf. 1:12–13), and he goes there to pray (cf. 1:35). He also finds the mountains as aesthetically conducive to prayer (cf. 3:13, 6:46; 9:2). Loving the sea, Jesus one time calms it (cf. 4:35–41) and at another time walks upon it (cf. 6:45–53).

Jesus appreciates the beauty of a good meal. Two times in Mark's Gospel he multiplies bread and fish to satisfy hungry crowds (cf. 6:30–44; 8:1–10). He also celebrates the passover meal with his friends (cf. 14:12–25), during which he gives his own body as food and his blood as drink to his disciples.

Jesus tells John: "Do not stop [the other exorcist]; for no one who does a deed of power in my name will be able soon afterward to speak evil of me. Whoever is not against us is for us" (Mark 9:39–40). In other words, he appreciates the beauty of another, who is not even a member of his group, enacting the kingdom of God.

Even though the author of Mark's Gospel portrays Jesus as knowing that the Temple will be destroyed by the Romans, Jesus enjoys the beauty of the building. After one of his disciples tells him, "Look, Teacher, what large stones and what large buildings!" (13:1), Jesus responds, "Do you see these great buildings? Not one stone will be left here upon another; all will be thrown down" (13:2).

Maybe Jesus' love of beauty shines through best in his ability to tell a good story. He tells parables about a sower and seed (cf. 4:1–9), about a lamp (cf. 4:21–25), about growing seed (cf. 4:26–29), about mustard seed (cf. 4:30–32), and about wicked tenant farmers (cf. 12:1–12). His stories often bring together two things that usually do not go together. How can twenty-five percent of seed produce a hundred percent crop? Who would plant a weed (mustard) in the garden? Jesus knew that a good story has the power to transform those with ears to hear it.

Jesus demonstrates how God can work in lives open and uncluttered by worldly concerns, in the lives of those who surrender themselves to unconditional love, to self-emptying love. God raised Jesus from the dead. Thus, the crowning of Jesus' humanity through death and resurrection will be the crowning of our humanity through death and resurrection. God validated Jesus' faithfulness by raising him from the dead. After all, that's what any authentic relationship accomplishes in two people—new life—as both continue to die to self in their individual and communal quest for self-discovery or transcendence. As Cook says, "It is in this man's (Jesus') whole life culminating in his death by crucifixion that we experience the true power of God."[31]

O'Grady states, "... The resurrection founds all our faith in the earthly Jesus as the human face of God."[32] Just as every act of Jesus manifested the divine, so does each individual in a relationship reveal one of the myriad possibilities of who God is. What happened to Jesus and his first followers continues to happen today. The heart of Jesus' personality consists of his relationship to God, and that example serves as a paradigm for the rest of humankind.

Jesus as Example of Friendship

The Markan account of Jesus' transfiguration provides an example of *friendshipping*. Mark's transfiguration account, misunderstood by Matthew and Luke who both copied and altered it, is a story revealing the author's understanding of resurrection, which follows Jesus' death. The interplay of death and resurrection forms the dialectic necessary for those relating. There can be no true freedom without dying to self by sharing self with another. Death liberates us for growth, so that we can become all that God wants us to be. It's only in losing life to another, that is, freely giving it away, that we actually find it and really live. That's why Jesus declares, "For those who want to save their life will lose it, and those who lose their life for my sake . . . will save it" (Mark 8:35), immediately before he experiences transfiguration.

Step 1: Always in Process

According to Mark, it was "six days" (9:2) after he had spoken those words that his transfiguration occurred. In biblical literature, six signifies incompleteness—in contrast to seven, signifying completeness. Any relationship is incomplete. The two people relating

31. Cook, *Christology*, 92.
32. O'Grady, *Models*, 46.

are always in process, individually and collectively. Who both are individually today are not who both will be individually tomorrow, and, consequently, who both will be collectively tomorrow.

Step 2: Continual Nurturance

". . . Jesus took with him Peter and James and John, and led them up a high mountain . . . ," says Mark (9:2). Relating is like climbing a mountain; it takes dedicated work. Two people do not really "fall in love." They may "fall in infatuation" or "fall in attraction," but they have to work at loving each other. Authentic *friendshipping* requires presence, openness, time, freedom, trust, communication, and sharing life experiences. A relationship that is always in process requires a decision from each person continually to foster and nurture it.

Step 3: Separateness and Togetherness

The Markan Jesus leads three of his disciples up a high mountain "apart, by themselves" (Mark 9:2). We find it most difficult "to relate" to another in the midst of a crowd. We need quality time "apart" or alone with the beloved, the person with whom we are *friendshipping*. Countless whole and healthy relationships come to an end because the two people fail to nurture sufficiently the necessary dialectic of separateness and togetherness pivotal to the ongoing process of relating.

Step 4: Constant Change

Alone, except for the presence of the one we love, the process of relating reveals and fosters transfiguration, change. Mark states that Jesus "was transfigured" before his three disciples (Mark 9:2). By making connections to each other through the seven aspects of human wholeness, we reveal how much we have changed from our last encounter with the beloved. Then, further change and development is fostered by the beloved. We are never ever the same. Process is part of our human nature. And because we are always in flux, we are always revealing who we are to the other so that he or she knows with whom he or she is relating.

Step 5: Transparency

Mark notes that as Jesus was transfigured, "his clothes became dazzling white, such as no one on earth could bleach them" (Mark 9:3). When white light is separated or refracted, its many shades can be seen. Two people relating serve as refractors for each other's white light. They become transparent so that they can see both themselves and the other. Their mutual transparency enables them to discover the Divine at work in their relationship and the transcendent character of it.

Step 6: Expanding Boundaries

People who are *friendshipping* enable each other to move their personal boundaries of self so that one knows the other even as he or she is being known by the other. In the Gospel of Mark's account of Jesus' transfiguration, Elijah and Moses appeared and talked with Jesus (cf. Mark 9:4). Mark portrays Jesus as crossing the boundary of death to the other side and entering into dialogue with the great prophet Elijah and the lawgiver Moses. Both Elijah and Moses, long thought to be dead, are alive. Expanding boundaries enables the dialectic of death-life, dying to self and rising to a new self.

Step 7: Beyond Plateau

After developing a relationship, we reach a point where we want to stay, a plateau experience. Peter tells Jesus, "Rabbi, it is good for us to be here; let us make three dwellings, one for you, one for Moses, and one for Elijah" (Mark 9:5). The plateau experience can be dangerous for a relationship. Why? Because the two people in it cease processing. They stop developing themselves in dialogue and dialectic with the beloved. Mutual enrichment and diminishment cease. After a while, relationships that have reached a plateau either get started again or they die. A relationship cannot exist on a plateau.

Step 8: Embracing Fear

There are ways to experience fear in a relationship. If it has reached a plateau, the fear may come in either having to jump-start it or watch it die. Fear enters into a relationship when an impasse is reached in terms of human disclosure. According to Mark, Peter did not know what he was saying because he and his two companions "were terrified" (Mark 9:6). When one person is unable to further disclose who he or she is in a friendship, communication ceases and words spoken by the other receive no response.

Friends may experience fear in the midst of encounter with the Divine. God's greatness may cause fear, yet it fills us with awe.

Step 9: Transcendence

In a healthy relationship, one that is always in the process of becoming, two people recognize the presence of God and hear the Holy One's voice through the other. ". . . A cloud overshadowed them, and from the cloud there came a voice," writes Mark (9:7). For those who relate, the other is the overshadowing cloud. The one person created in the image of God meets another person created in the image of God, and the Holy One meets the Holy One through human friendships.

God is revealed through human friendships. Each person shares God's grace with the other, and, in so doing, enables the other to hear and clarify God's voice breaking through the words of the beloved: This is my son or daughter, the beloved, listen to him or her (Mark 9:7). Friends are aware of the immediate consciousness of God, and, through each other, they mediate life itself to the other.

Step 10: Encountering the Divine in the Ordinary

Once the experience of *friendshipping* is begun, both people realize that they must return to daily life. Then, when both return to the work of relating, they will discover that they have been enriched by the ordinary. No matter what the depth of love shared or the degree of connection accomplished in the areas of wholeness, both people must return to the normal world. That's why Mark tells the reader that Jesus' transfiguration ends as abruptly as it began. Suddenly, when the three disciples looked around, "they saw no one with them any more, but only Jesus" (Mark 9:8). Then, they come down the mountain. By returning to the ordinary details of daily living, both persons interact with others and bring the fruit of those encounters to share with the person with whom they *friendship*.

Step 11: Ripple Effect

While we have a tendency to think that relationship affects only the two people involved in it, it has much wider implications. One relationship between two people affects their communities of work, family, recreation, prayer, politics, social, etc.

A relationship affects other groups with whom both persons are involved. A relationship always in the process of moving towards human wholeness brings its richness and depth to share with others in varying and unique ways, even as others are having the same effect on the two in their relationship. In other words, the dialectic of enrichment and diminishment is at work both for the two people and for each of them and the communities to which each belongs.

The always-emerging quality of friendship means that it is greater than the two people who are involved in it. That is why Paul tells the Corinthians they are individually members of each other (cf. 1 Cor 12:27). A community is composed of many members, who function as one body. What each of the members does or doesn't do affects the community. In his letter to the Romans, Paul makes this clearer, stating, that "individually we are members one of another" (12:5).

The human wholeness that is the result of two people relating draws in other individuals and affects them individually and collectively. Thus, through their relating with others, many others are affected, like ripples on a pond when a stone is tossed in. The experiences of relating with others in any number of communities are brought back to enhance the wholeness of the relationship with the beloved.

A web of relationships is enhanced by every healthy one and harmed by every unhealthy one. The human wholeness of one overflows and affects the human wholeness of many to some degree, or the lack of human wholeness harms others. Even as one person is always in the process of change and development, and even as two in a relationship are always in the process of change and development, so are communities to which both belong individually and collectively always in the process of change and development. Likewise, the web of communities is always in the process of change and development.

Questions for Reflection and Discussion

1. How does the paradigm of Jesus as an example of human wholeness through relationship affect you?

2. How is one of your friendships a direct experience of God? Explain.

3. Besides Jesus, who else might serve as a model of human wholeness? Explain.

4. How does the transfiguration narrative serve as a model for your friendship? Apply the eleven steps of the friendship model to one of your relationships. What do you discover?

5. What ripple effects in your broader community do you see stemming from your friendships?

6. Are you experiencing human wholeness in your relationships? In what healthy relationships will you invest more? What unhealthy relationships will you reassess?

Bibliography

Buber, Martin. *I & Thou*. New York: Charles Scribner's Sons, 1970.

Chittister, Joan. "The Monastic Way." (February 2000).

Coll, Regina A. *Christianity & Feminism in Conversation*. Mystic, CT: Twenty-Third, 1994.

Cook, Michael L. *Christology as Narrative Quest*. Collegeville, MN: Liturgical Press, 1997.

Covey, Stephen R. *Daily Reflections for Highly Effective People*. New York: Simon & Schuster, 1994.

DeMello, Anthony. *One Minute Wisdom*. Garden City, NY: Doubleday, 1985.

Dorr, Donal. *Integral Spirituality*. Maryknoll, NY: Orbis, 1990.

Dyer, George. "What Happens at Mass is More Than Meets the Eye." *U.S. Catholic* 63:3 (1998) 28–33.

Elshtain, Jean Bethke. "Families and Trust: Connecting Private Lines to Civic Goals." *Chicago Studies* 39:1 (2000) 17–26.

Fowler, James W. *Becoming Adult, Becoming Christian*. San Francisco: Harper & Row, 1984.

———. *Stages of Faith*. San Francisco: Harper & Row, 1981.

Haughey, John C. "Toward a Pneumatology of Lay Ministry." *Chicago Studies* 39:1 (2000) 27–46.

Holy Spirit, Lord and Giver of Life, The. Translated by Agostino Bono. New York: Crossroad, 1997.

Huebsch, Bill. *A New Look at Grace: A Spirituality of Wholeness*. Mystic, CT: Twenty-Third, 1988.

Ludwig, Robert A. *Grace and Christ: Fundamental Theology and the Meaning of Salvation*. The Loyola Institute for Ministry Extension Program. New Orleans: Loyola University Press, 1995.

Merton, Thomas. *The Intimate Merton: His Life from His Journals*. Edited by Patrick Hart and Jonathan Montaldo. New York: Harper Collins, 1999.

Mitchell, Nathan. "The Amen Corner." *Worship* 73:3 (1999) 249–59.

Morneau, Robert. "How Does Our Garden Grow?" *U.S. Catholic* 64:6 (1999) 34–37.

Bibliography

O'Day, Gail R., and David Peterson, eds. *The Access Bible: New Revised Standard Version with the Apocryphal/Deuterocanonical Books.* New York: Oxford University Press, 1999.

O'Grady, John F. *Models of Jesus.* Garden City, NY: Doubleday, 1981. Reprinted by the Loyola Institute for Ministry Extension Program. New Orleans: Loyola University Press, 1989.

Powell, John. "Thou Shalt Know Thyself." *U.S. Catholic* 64:4 (1999) 28–33.

Shea, John. *Elijah at the Wedding Feast and Other Tales.* Chicago: ACTA, 1999.

_____"Eucharist: Broken Bread Makes Us Whole." *U.S. Catholic* 63:2 (1998) 10–16.

Shlain, Leonard. *The Alphabet Versus the Goddess.* New York: Viking, 1998.

Teasdale, Wayne. *The Mystic Heart.* Novato, CA: New World Library, 1999.

www.ingramcontent.com/pod-product-compliance
Lightning Source LLC
Chambersburg PA
CBHW071107090426
42737CB00013B/2517